THREE POPULAR FRENCH COMEDIES

Three Popular French Comedies

Translations and Notes by
ALBERT BERMEL

Frederick Ungar Publishing Co.
New York

Copyright © 1960, 1961, 1975 by Albert Bermel and
    Joyce Bermel
Printed in the United States of America
Library of Congress Catalog Card Number 75-1959
ISBN 0-8044-2041-6 (cloth)
ISBN 0-8044-6044-2 (paper)

CONTENTS

INTRODUCTION
French Comic Theater

We think of France as being pre-eminently the land of the avant-garde in art. In the past twenty-five years Butor, Sarraute, Simon, and others have reshaped the novel, while Sartre, Beckett, Ionesco, Adamov, and Genet worked transformations in the content and textures of plays. Before them, Artaud, the Surrealists, Giraudoux, and Cocteau, preceded in their turn by Apollinaire, Jarry, and directors like Paul Fort, wrought their own drastic surprises. And before *them* the French impressionists opened new adventures in painting and design. In addition, France has been quick to pick up and welcome artistic experiments and experimenters from abroad —Pirandello, Picasso, Strindberg, Gombrowicz, Stravinsky, and countless others, usually before they have consolidated their reputations.

But France is also, in its paradoxical fashion, a country of persistent tradition. Montaigne, Pascal, La Fontaine, Racine, Corneille, Molière, and other authors distant by at least three centuries are still artistically alive, kicking, and undergoing constant re-examination of a salutary, nonmedical kind. Most of the leading publishers in Paris carry comprehensive series of critical studies and frequently revised editions of what have become classics. The continuity of French traditionalism enables one to put together in a book like this three plays from the eighteenth, nineteenth, and turn of the twentieth centuries without needing to justify the choice by saying they offer interesting contrasts. It does not diminish the individuality of Beaumarchais, Labiche, or Courteline to mention that each was unavoidably in debt over his ears to Molière, any more than we diminish Molière by drawing up a reckoning of his obligations to the commedia dell'arte, Plautus, Terence, and French folk drama.

Comedy draws repeatedly and unashamedly on popular dramatic situations, character types, and themes. This is equally true of film comedies, such as Chaplin's, Keaton's, and Lloyd's, and it is even true of comedies of manners, such as those of the Restoration playwrights, and of Wilde, Shaw, Jones, Pinero, and Sheridan, which may have high-society settings but feed on age-old coincidences, reversals, surprises, mistaken identities, reconciliations, and power ploys. Comedy constantly goes back to the popular theater to refresh—if not remake—itself. I use the word *popular* to mean having an appeal, not so much to large numbers of people as to many different segments of a populace, a spectrum of classes and tastes. In this sense the Old Vic in London was always a popular theater, and so is the New York Shakespeare Festival. Molière's plays, designed for several Court productions at one of Louis XIV's palaces, then came into Paris and played to the general public after only light modifications in the staging. The Elizabethan and Jacobean plays transferred each winter from the "public" outdoor theaters to the "private" ones indoors. In France the plays of Beaumarchais, Labiche, and Courteline were popular in both senses, and they have remained so. The general public likes them as sheer entertainment, yet intellectuals and critics respect them because, like any durable art, they improve with further acquaintance. The craftsmanship in a brief play like *The Commissioner Has a Big Heart* makes it a model of dramaturgy: not merely is it a technical feat; it is crammed with fascinating, satirical observations, ideas, and character quirks that cannot be assimilated on a first reading or viewing.

The Barber of Seville's popularity has been slightly dimmed by that of its offspring, Rossini's opera, which seems to be on display everywhere all the time. But the parent play has its own delights to offer. Beaumarchais, snubbed as an upstart by the courtiers of Louis XV and Louis XVI (see biographical note), took his historic revenge by poking fun at nobility and its hangers-on by making his hero a lowborn barber-valet. The setting may be southern Spain but the references are unmistakably French. Figaro (the name is thought to be taken from *fi*, the French word for "fie," and *Caron*, Beaumarchais's family name) is very likely the author's mischievous version of himself, a commoner, a jack of all trades and master of most of them, a servant with the mental agility to rescue himself from one sticky situation after another. Count Almaviva, for all that he is the nominal hero-lover, is an aristocrat and therefore inept when he is not operating on Figaro's instructions.

The slow-witted master and his resourceful servant go back at least as far as the early Roman comedies. There is a striking parallel, though, between Beaumarchais's main plot and Molière's in *L'Étourdi (The Blunderer)*, in which the master, Lélie, continually wrecks his chances of winning the heroine while his valet, Mascarille, has to cope with the obstacles that Lélie stupidly sets up against himself.

The "characters" in the play are Figaro and the doctor, whose name, Bartholo, comes from Pantaloon, the old Venetian cuckold of Italian comedy. Almaviva ("long live honor!") is a stock figure, the susceptible, dashing dunce with a military air, who becomes much more compelling when he pretends to be someone else, the horse doctor or the music teacher, and acquires something of Figaro's vivacity during these scenes: masked, he takes on new personality and not just *a* new personality. Rosine is a conventionally harmless and shockable ingénue; evidently all that the playwright expected of the actress was beauty, graceful movement, gasps, sighs, hints of coquettishness, and horrified asides. Bartholo's two servants, Puberty *(La Jeunesse)* and Lively *(L'Éveillé)* are tugged in and out of the action for quick laughs, but another minor character, Don Bazile, is the center of one of the brightest scenes in the comic French drama.

The plotting in *The Barber* is elegant, a reassuring experience for actors and spectators who want every exit and entrance to be defensible; the structure of each act is firm; and the play canters to its conclusion, hardly slowing up when it delivers a kick at hack playwrights here and at doctors there and at nobility most of the time. With its successor, *The Marriage of Figaro, The Barber* contributed to an emotional climate of protest and defiance that made the French Revolution possible.

The comic effects conjured up by Labiche lie, as Bergson pointed out in *Le Rire* ("Laughter"), somewhere "between very rough and very refined amusement," veering now toward one extreme, now toward the other. *Pots of Money* is an epic comedy of complications, not of character. Certain bizarre *characteristics* do amuse us, for instance, Boursey's disposition to go through life striking noble platitudes; the affection of Danne, the farmer, for dung; the anxieties of Leonida and Corden to find marriage partners who will be soul mates and ensure their "future happiness"; and the determination of Poche, the marriage broker, to please everybody except his employees. But these are theatrical by-products, twitches set up by the pervasive movement of the play, which consists of one escape after another, a search for refuge in a hostile city. Being a humorist, and therefore malicious, Labiche took pleasure in embarrassing each of his characters in turn. Being a good-natured man, he got them out of trouble by the final curtain. Being a realist, he did not attempt to slap a happy ending on all their lives—by, for example, uniting Leonida and Corden. Modern theatergoers, who are accustomed to sucking a moral out of even (that is, especially) the flimsiest comedies, are entitled to ask, after the capers are over, what Labiche and his collaborator Delacour were getting at. The answer: his audiences, who saw themselves locked in jail with nothing to free themselves with but a pickax and a song, or taken for a gang of jewel thieves, or trapped in a restaurant with insufficient cash after misreading the prices on the menu. And how did these audiences respond? With catcalls? Just the reverse. The more Labiche mocked them and punctured their pretenses by showing them caricatures of themselves and their neighbors in ridiculous plights, the more they cheered.

There is then social comment in Labiche, but it is subordinated. However, in a 1972 revival entitled *The Piggy Bank* and directed by Peter Stein in West Berlin, Labiche's social satire was subtly brought out; the production won praise from several of the more intelligent reviewers who discerned in the text a devastatingly critical, and at the same time, fond, picture of the French petty bourgeoisie in the nineteenth century—and the twentieth.

In every one of the five acts Labiche leaves comedy behind and strikes out into the perilous terrain of farce. Courteline, in *The Commissioner Has a Big Heart*, heaps up the farce from one end of the play to the other. He underlines his farcical intent in the final scene and still more firmly in the final line. The Commissioner, after his humiliations at the hands of Floche, is released from a coal box by his subordinates, who cannot hide their satisfaction. Covered in coal dust and reft of his dignity, he bellows: "There's a maniac at large!" So there is. The Commissioner. Through the play we have watched this vindictive paper-shuffler putting down people who come to him for help, and holding on with maniacal ferocity to his role as Big Chief in the community. Courteline, who had more than a passing hatred for blinkered authority, exposes this tyrant to a violent dose of imagination in the person of Floche. The latter, believing that the universe has a spider on its ceiling, a bug in its bedstead, and a rat in its bass violin, today strikes us as being anything but mad. Nature still imitates art. It probably always did.

Albert Bermel

Herbert H. Lehman College, 1975

PIERRE-AUGUSTIN CARON DE BEAUMARCHAIS
(1732–1799)

Like Molière and Voltaire before him and Courteline after him, Beaumarchais chose his own surname; he also gave it aristocratic coinage by prefacing it with a "de," which he dropped after the French Revolution. His father was André Caron, a watchmaker to the king, with a modest establishment in the Rue St. Denis, slightly north of the Île de la Cité in Paris. (Today, just under a mile to the east, and running parallel, is the Boulevard Beaumarchais.) Pierre Caron attended boarding school each morning, without distinguishing himself, and took religious instruction each afternoon, without becoming particularly pious. At thirteen, he was confirmed and left school to work for his father. Occasionally, he sold watches without telling his father; he also ran about with a fast crowd of youngsters during working hours and in the evening, and while at his watchmaker's bench taught himself music: the harp, the violin, and the flute. His father, after three years, was goaded into banishing him from the house and business, and let him return only after Pierre signed a six-point treaty of good behavior.

From then on, he rallied himself and settled down to study (in his own time) the great French writers, mathematics, and mechanics. When he was twenty-one, he developed a new, simplified watch escapement; he showed it to a rival watchmaker named Lepaute who admired it so much that he appropriated the idea. Pierre submitted this case of infraction to the Royal Academy of Sciences, and won. Following the public interest that the case aroused, he sought and gained the title Watchmaker to the King, and confirmed his reputation for ingenuity by constructing "the smallest watch ever made," which he set in a ring and sold to Mme. de Pompadour.

Not long after this he met the young wife of an old man, Francquet, a Controller of the Royal Kitchen, or rather, she introduced herself to him by dropping her watch and taking it to him for repair. She was rapidly smitten by Caron's good looks and confident presence and not only took him to her husband, but persuaded that gentleman to pass on his duties and title to the young watchmaker. In January 1756 old Francquet died and ten months later, when the Francquet estate had been settled on the widow, with the assistance of Beaumarchais and his lawyer, he married her and moved into her luxurious, well-servanted quarters in Versailles, near the palace. From now on, he added "de Beaumarchais" to his name and proceeded to step lightly in court circles.

The following year his wife contracted typhus and died suddenly. Beaumarchais had to return his wife's property to her first husband's relatives, but managed to retain his court appointment by teaching music to the two daughters of Louis XV. He combined this work with a high-sounding position, the duties of which were to prosecute rabbit poachers on the king's preserves. In the few cases of prosecution that he undertook, Beaumarchais showed formidable skill in law and oratory, which in France are perhaps the same thing. His official functions, however, did not prevent him from enjoying liaisons with several ladies, from indulging in duels (in one he killed a knight, in another he wounded a marquis), and from provoking envy at court.

In 1764 he went to Spain to shame a grandee who had "compromised" one of his two sisters living in Madrid. The shaming over, he stayed in Spain for a further eleven months, making the cultural rounds and meeting Iberian ladies, one of whom he presented to the Spanish king, Charles III, with beneficial results all around.

Back in Paris, he wrote his first play, *Eugenia,* a melodramatic comedy of court intrigue, which took him seven versions to get right. It was performed in 1767 at the Théâtre-Français and caused some bad feeling which, together with sharply worded whispers that were circulated by other members of court society, alienated him from Louis XV.

In April 1768 he married a young widow, who eight months later gave birth to a son. Beaumarchais then went to work on his second play, *The Two Friends,* or *The Merchant of Lyon,* which was produced and generally disapproved of in 1770. On the poster outside the theater, a disappointed spectator wrote under the title *The Two Friends:* "by a man who has none."

In November of that same year his second wife died, and his son survived her by only two years. During this wrecking of his personal life, Beaumarchais had been polishing the draft of a comic opera, *The Barber of Seville.* By 1774 the play was ready for staging, but during that year Beaumarchais engaged in a drawn-out and complicated litigation, which began when he attempted to recover some money owed to him and ended in name-slinging and a public scandal with many prominent people maligned. Beaumarchais lost, was deprived of his civil rights, and, in spite of the sympathy of such men as Voltaire and Rousseau, decided to go to England and let a few tempers cool off.

By carrying out certain duties for Louis XV and his grandson and successor, Louis XVI—principally by suppressing certain libels being written about the French royal family in England—Beaumarchais vindicated himself and returned to France. In 1775 *The Barber,* which in its musical form had been rejected by the Italian Players, was mounted as a five-act play. But the audience grew restless during the fifth act; Beaumarchais thereupon cut, scraped, sharpened, and generally improved the text, reducing it to four acts. "I removed," he said, "the fifth wheel from the chariot." Three days later, the second performance was a triumph. There were fewer digs, but the ones left penetrated deeper.

Beaumarchais then took off again for England, to pay off the ambisexual Chevalier d'Eon, who was threatening to publish libels against the king, and sullying the fair name of France by appearing alternately in men's and women's clothes. While in England, Beaumarchais conspired with various American representatives and, for the sake of France's sugar islands, extracted one million francs from Louis XVI to assist the revolutionaries in the then British colony. In the year that followed, he set up a trading company of his own and sent munitions and materials to the value of six million francs to America, most of which was never repaid. A warship that he had outfitted especially to convoy the goods across the Atlantic was captured by the British. Altogether he lost about four million francs on his American dealings. At the same time—his credit was still good—he was making regular loans to a number of friends, including an impoverished prince and princess who understandably addressed him as BONmarchais.

His next enterprise was to set up a printing firm to publish the complete works of Voltaire in a luxury edition of seventy-two volumes. This took him a number of years, but the complete works eventually appeared, at a further, enormous loss to Beaumarchais.

In 1781 *The Marriage of Figaro,* Beaumarchais's successor to *The Barber,* was accepted by the Théâtre-Français, but Louis XVI, who had heard a reading of the play and hated it, canceled the performance thirty minutes before the curtain

was due to rise. The play was not performed for another
three years; then it was a rousing success. Mozart started to
write his opera based on it that same year.

Beaumarchais's third marriage, to a Mlle. Villermawlaz
(they already had a daughter aged eight), came in the middle of more court cases, this time against him, for slander,
but the prosecution's arguments were obviously based on
malice, and Beaumarchais won. Somehow surviving more un-
profitable business deals, he came intact through the French
Revolution, which began in 1789; he was sympathetic to its
aims and took part in it eagerly as an adviser to the Commune, but as a professed former nobleman he was suspect:
his house was raided several times; he was imprisoned and
freed and finally fled to England, where a businessman to
whom he owed money had him sent to debtors' prison.

In his cell he wrote *Six Epochs, the Most Painful Nine
Months of My Life,* which he smuggled out; it was published in France and helped to raise enough money to get
him out of jail. He returned home and almost immediately
was sent abroad again as a Commissioner of the Republic;
while he was out of the country, his enemies managed to get
him branded as an *émigré,* an enemy of the regime, who
had fled out of the country. Seals were placed on his property
six times and six times they were removed. He was "investi-
gated" five times and five times he was cleared, largely owing
to the efforts of his wife, who had remained in France with
their daughter. During this time, Beaumarchais traveled
penuriously through England, Holland, and northern
Germany. In 1796 the "erasure" of his name as an *émigré,*
once and for all, meant that he could come back to Paris and
join his wife and daughter and his daughter's fiancé.

At sixty-four, although he was slower on his feet and with
his tongue, and although he was now deaf enough to need
an ear trumpet, Beaumarchais settled into something like his
old, hectic life, helping to produce his plays, writing letters
on dozens of topics to dozens of people, including members
of the American Congress which had failed to recognize its
old debts to him. His last play had been *The Guilty Mother,*
which featured the same characters as *The Marriage,* but
now older, wiser, more serious and more dull. It had flopped
in 1792 on its first production, but was revived several times
with varying receptions.

In the midst of this new whirl of activities, on the night
of 17-18 May 1799, Beaumarchais died in his bed of an
apoplectic stroke, at the age of sixty-seven. According to his
friend Gudin, his face was set in a peaceful half-smile.

A LIST OF BEAUMARCHAIS'S PLAYS:

Eugenia (1766); *The Two Friends* (1770); *The Barber of Seville* (1775); *The Marriage of Figaro* (1781); *Tarare,* an opera (1785); *The Guilty Mother* (1786).

SUGGESTIONS FOR FURTHER READING ON BEAUMARCHAIS:

Dalsemé, René. *Beaumarchais.* Trans. by Hannaford Bennett. New York: G. P. Putnam's Sons, 1929.

Hall, Evelyn Beatrice. *The Friends of Voltaire.* New York: G. P. Putnam's Sons, 1907.

Kite, Elizabeth. *Beaumarchais and the War of American Independence.* Boston: Richard G. Badger (The Gorham Press), 1918.

de Loménie, Louis Leonard. *Beaumarchais and His Times.* Trans. by Henry S. Edwards. New York: Harper's, 1857.

Newman, Ernest. *Great Operas,* Vol. I, pp. 34-74, *The Barber of Seville.* New York: Random House, Inc. (Vintage Books, Inc.), 1958.

Rivers, John. *Figaro, The Life of Beaumarchais.* London: Hutchinson, 1922.

IN FRENCH ONLY:

Bailly, Auguste. *Beaumarchais.* Paris: Fayard, 1945.

Latzarus, Louis. *Beaumarchais.* Paris: Plon, 1930.

Le Barbier de Sèville and *Le Mariage de Figaro,* texts with notes, published in the Classiques Larousse edition.

A LETTER FROM
BEAUMARCHAIS TO THE READER [1]

The author, modestly dressed, bows, and presents his play to the reader.

Sir:

I have the honor to offer you a new little work of my own creation. I would like to catch you in one of those happy moments when you are free from cares, content with your health, your business, your mistress, your dinner, your stomach, and you can delight for a moment in reading my *Barber of Seville;* for only under these conditions will you be an amusable man and an indulgent reader.

But if some accident has impaired your health; if your business is not going well; if your beauty has been false to her promises; if your dinner was bad, or your digestion difficult, pray put my *Barber* to one side; the moment is not right for it: examine your accounts, study your adversary's brief, reread that treacherous, secret note addressed to your Rose, or peruse Tissot's masterpieces [2] on temperance and reflect on their political, economic, dietetic, philosophic, or moral values. . . .

Beaumarchais' Dramatic Theories

. . . I have been heartily assured that when an author emerged broken-backed but triumphant in the theater, all that he needed, sir, was to be approved by you and torn to pieces by a few newspapers in order to have won every literary laurel. Thus my glory is assured if you are good enough to grant me the laurels of your approval, for I am given to understand that a few reviewers will not refuse me their abuse.

[1] From "A Temperate Letter on the Failure and the Criticism of *The Barber of Seville,*" written as a prefatory note to the play in its first published edition, 1775. *Ed.*

[2] Tissot was a contemporary of Beaumarchais and wrote popularized books on medicine. *Ed.*

Already one of them, employed by *Bouillon*,[3] has honored me by assuring his subscribers that my play was without plan, without unity, without characters, void of intrigue, and bereft of comedy.

Another reviewer, who is even more naïve, gave a frank account of my play, then added to his critical laurel this flattering praise of my person: "The reputation of M. Beaumarchais has indeed sunk, and honest people are convinced at last that once the peacock's feathers are plucked from him, only a nasty, black, brazen, voracious crow will remain. . . ."

Vicissitudes of "The Barber" and of Theater in General

. . . That is how men are: if you are successful, they welcome you, support you, pet you, they are honored to know you; but beware of stumbling in your career: at the slightest setback, my dear friends, remember that there *are* no more friends.

And that is exactly what happened to us the day after that saddest of opening nights. You would have seen the *Barber's* faint friends scatter, hide their faces, or flee; the women, who are normally so brave and protective, sink into their hoods up to their feathered hairdos and lower their eyes in confusion; the men run around to each other, publicly apologizing for the good things they had said about my play, and blaming my accursed first reading for all the false pleasures they had tasted. It was a case of total desertion, absolute abandonment.

Some men turned their eyes to the left as I passed on the right, affecting not to see me. Others with more courage—first making very sure that no one was watching—dragged me into a corner and said: "How did you manage to put that illusion over on us? For you must agree, my friend, that your play is the flattest platitude in the world."

"Alas, gentlemen, I read my platitude quite as flatly as I wrote it, but in the name of your goodness in speaking to me again after my disgrace, and to uphold your second judgment, do not allow the play to be repeated on the stage; for if, by mischance, it were played as I read it, you would perhaps be deluded anew, and you would be angry at me in no longer knowing when you were right and when wrong. God forbid that."

Not one of them believed me. They let the play be performed again, and for once I was a prophet in my own coun-

[3] A contemporary journal. *Ed.*

try. Poor Figaro, beaten down by the muttering of the league of critics and almost buried on Friday,[4] did not behave like Candide: my hero took heart and on Sunday he rose again. And his vitality could not be weakened by fasting through an entire Lent or by the hardships of seventeen public performances. But who knows how long this will last? Our nation is so fickle and giddy that I would not want to swear that people will even be aware of Figaro in five or six centuries.

Plays, gentlemen, are to their authors what children are to women: they cost more pain than they give pleasure. Follow their careers: no sooner do they see the light of day than a swollen style is detected and hot censorship has to be applied; some of them have never recovered from it. Instead of treating them gently, the cruel pit bullies them and knocks them down. And often, while the actor is supposed to be cradling them, he injures them. Lose sight of them for an instant and you find them—alas!—lying about all over the place, tattered and disfigured, with sections nibbled out of them, and covered with criticisms. If they escape all these ills and illuminate the world for one moment, they are overtaken by the most deadly fate of all —oblivion. They sink into the abyss and are lost forever in the vast tomb of dead books. . . .

What Criticism Should Be—What It Is

Let us see, if you will, whether the reporter from *Bouillon* observed in his review the friendly nature and especially the candor which are the marks of good criticism.

"The play is a farce," he said.

So let us ignore all its qualities. The bad name a foreign cook gives to French stews does not change their flavor; it is only when they fall into his hands that the stews lose their taste. Let us analyze what *Bouillon* calls farce.

"The play," he said, "has no plan."

Is it because the plan is too simple that it escapes the wisdom of this adolescent reviewer?

An amorous old man intends to marry his ward on the following day; a young man who is more clever forestalls him, and on that very day captures the girl in the guardian's house, right under his nose, and makes her his wife. There you have the foundation on which a comedy, a tragedy, a drama, or an opera could be built with equal success. Is Molière's *Miser* anything else? Or [Racine's] *Mithridates?*

---

4 Opening night, February 23, 1775. *Ed.*

The classification of a play, like that of any other work, depends less on its plot than on the characters who put that plot into action. As for me, all I wanted to build on this foundation was a lighthearted, amusing play, an intrigue. I had no need of a black villain; it was enough for my schemer to be a comic, happy-go-lucky fellow who laughs equally at the success and failure of his enterprises. Thus the work, instead of developing as a serious drama, turned into a very gay comedy. And because the guardian is a little less stupid than those who are usually deceived in the theater, the play has more action and, more important, the schemers need to be more resourceful.

Reply to Some Objections

"The play is a series of improbabilities," continues this journalist, who is an accredited and privileged writer for *Bouillon*.

"Improbabilities!" . . . Let us look into them, just for enjoyment.

His Excellency Count Almaviva, whose intimate friend I am honored to have been for a long time, is a young lord, or rather, was, for age and responsible duties have since transformed him into a very grave man, such as I have become myself. His Excellency was, then, a young Spanish lord, as vital and passionate as all the lovers of his nation, which is thought to be cold but is merely lazy.

He had been secretly pursuing a beautiful lady whom he had caught a glimpse of in Madrid and whose guardian had swiftly brought her home. One morning, as he was walking beneath her windows, in Seville, where he had been trying for a week to attract her attention, chance brought Figaro the barber to the same spot.

"Ah, chance," my critic will say, "and if chance had not brought the barber to that spot on that day, what would become of the play?"

"It would have begun, my friend, at some other time."

"Impossible. According to you, the guardian was getting married the next day."

"Then there wouldn't be any play; or if there had, it would have been different. Is a thing improbable because it could have happened otherwise? . . ."

. . . Chance, then, brings Figaro the barber to this same spot; he is a good talker, a bad poet, a daring musician, a guitar-slapper, and the count's former valet. He is established now in Seville, is equally successful with beards, romances, and marriages, and wields the barber's lancet as adroitly as the druggist's pump. He is the terror of husbands, the darling of wives, and exactly the man we were looking for. Investigation shows that what we call passion is nothing but desire inflamed by obstacles; thus our young lover might have been content merely to dream about a beautiful woman if he had met her in society, but because she was imprisoned and it was impossible for him to marry her— he fell in love.

But to recite the entire play to you here, sir, would be to question your wisdom. . . . You will certainly see that "all the troubles the count has to go to" are *not* "simply to allow him to put back a letter," which is only a property in the plot. He is trying to break into a stronghold defended by a vigilant, suspicious old guardian; to fool a man who catches on to every maneuver right away, and obliges his enemy to operate rather slowly so as not to be defeated on the first try.

And when you realize that the whole idea of the denouement is that the guardian has locked his door and given his passkey to Bazile, so that only the two of them can enter for the marriage later, you can only be astonished that such an honest critic toys with his reader's trust, or is mistaken, when he writes: "The count takes the trouble to reach the balcony with Figaro by climbing a ladder, although the door is not locked."

And when, finally, you see the unfortunate guardian who was betrayed by his very precautions, compelled to sign the count's marriage contract and to sanction what he was not able to prevent—you will leave it to the critic to decide this question: Was that guardian an "imbecile" for not understanding an intrigue that was completely hidden from him, when the critic himself, from whom nothing was hidden, was not able to understand any better?

If the critic *had* followed the plot would he still have neglected all the good things in the work?

I can forgive him for not noticing how the first act brightly introduces and displays the characters.

I am sympathetic that he found no trace of comedy in the big second-act scene where the girl manages to mislead her mistrustful, angry guardian about a letter delivered in his presence, and to make him ask pardon on his knees for his suspicions.

I am not at all surprised that he did not say a single word about the third-act scene of Bazile's stupefaction, which seemed to be such a novelty in the theater and entertained so many spectators.

I will even overlook his failure to suspect that the author had deliberately plunged into a last-act predicament, by having the ward confess to her guardian that the count had stolen the key, a predicament that the author unscrambles in two words, and for a playful moment gives his audience something new to worry about.

I accept his failure to see that although this is one of the liveliest plays in the theater, it was written without the least equivocation, without one thought, one single word which would alarm even the modesty of the nobility in their enclosed boxes.[5] Nevertheless, all this is something of a feat, sir, in a century when respectability has become almost as hypocritical as morals have become relaxed. I grant your point. Naturally, none of this is worth the attention of such an important critic.

But how is it that he could not admire something that made every virtuous man in the audience spill tears of tenderness and pleasure? I mean the filial piety of Figaro, who could not forget his mother: "You know this guardian then?" the count says to him in the first act. "Like my own mother," Figaro replies. A miser would have said: "Like my pockets." A dandy would have answered: "Like myself." An ambitious man: "Like the road to Versailles." And the journalist from *Bouillon:* "Like my bookseller"—Each man's comparisons centering on the object that interests him most.

"Like my own mother," said the tender and respectful son.

Let us pass silently over his sharp reproach to the young lady, for having "all the faults of a badly bred girl." True, he does try to avoid stating the consequences of the imputation by blaming it on others: he employs that banal, impersonal phrase—as if somebody else had written it—"One finds in the young lady," etc. One finds!

What did he want her to do? Instead of yielding to a very likable young lover who proves to be a titled man of quality, should our charming young lady marry the gouty old doctor? A fine future he has planned for her! And because she is not of Monsieur's opinion, she has "all the faults of a badly bred girl!"

Some knowing people noticed that I had fallen into the mistake of criticizing and poking fun at French customs in a play set in Seville, when, for the sake of consistency, I

---

[5] *Petites loges,* boxes behind the orchestra from which one could observe without being observed. *Ed.*

should have concentrated on Spanish customs. They are right: I had thought about that and to bring the believability nearer perfection, I had at first resolved to write the play and have it performed in the Spanish language; but a man of taste pointed out to me that it would perhaps lose a little of its gaiety for the Parisian public, which made me decide to write it in French. You can see that I made a multitude of sacrifices for the sake of gaiety, but did not succeed in loosening the frown on the face of *Bouillon*'s reviewer.

Another amateur [playwright] seized on a moment when many people were in the lobby to reproach me in the gravest tone because my play resembled *You Can't Think of Everything.*[6]

"Resemble, sir! I maintain that my play IS *You Can't Think of Everything.*"

"How is that?"

"Well, sir, you haven't yet thought of everything in my play."

The amateur stopped short and everyone laughed much more to think that the man who reproached me about *You Can't Think of Everything* is a man who has never thought of a single thing.

A few days after (this is more serious), at the house of a lady who was indisposed, a solemn gentleman—black suit, hair on end, the head of his cane forming a crow's beak which brushed the lady's hand—courteously offered several misgivings concerning the accuracy of the arrows which I let fly at doctors.

"Sir," I said to him, "are you a friend of one of them? I should be deeply sorry if a mere flippant remark . . ."

"Not at all: I see that you don't know me; I never take anyone's side; I am speaking now on behalf of medical practitioners in general."

I tried hard to imagine who this man might be. "In the case of humor," I added, "you know, sir, that people never ask if the story is true, only if it is good."

"Do you think you will fare any better in this discussion than you did in the earlier ones?"

"Admirably put, Doctor," said the lady. "What a monster he is! Daring to speak so badly of us. Let us join forces."

At the word "doctor," I knew that she was speaking to her private physician.

"It is true, dear lady and sir," I replied modestly, "that I have permitted myself a few trifling errors, for the lighter

---

6 Comic opera by Sedaine and Monsigny. *Ed.*

they are, the less grave their consequences. After all, there are two powerful groups whose influence is felt throughout the universe and who share the world—and nobody can dethrone them, not even the envious among us: beautiful women will always reign through pleasure and doctors through pain; and radiant health will let us conquer love, just as sickness will make us surrender to medicine. . . ."

Conclusion

But I am drifting too far from my subject. Let us return to *The Barber of Seville*. Or on second thoughts, sir, let us not return. Enough has been said about a romp. Without realizing it, I could fall into the error for which we Frenchmen are rightly reproached: of always writing frivolous verses about major concerns and huge dissertations on minor ones.

I am, sir, Your most respectful, humble and obedient servant,

The Author.

Translated by Joyce Bermel

THE BARBER OF SEVILLE

OR THE USELESS PRECAUTION

by Pierre-Augustin Caron de Beaumarchais

FIRST PERFORMED AT THE COMÉDIE-FRANÇAISE
ON FEBRUARY 23, 1775

CHARACTERS

COUNT ALMAVIVA, a Spanish grandee
DR. BARTHOLO, guardian of Rosine
ROSINE, young lady of noble birth, ward of Bartholo
FIGARO, a barber, former valet of Almaviva
DON BAZILE, an organist, Rosine's singing teacher
PUBERTY (LA JEUNESSE), an old servant of Bartholo
LIVELY (L'ÉVEILLÉ), a young servant of Bartholo
A NOTARY
AN ALCALDE or Spanish magistrate
POLICEMEN and other SERVANTS

ACT I

(The stage represents a street in Seville, with grilled windows; THE COUNT *is alone, pacing to and fro, dressed in a flowing brown cloak and low-brimmed hat. He takes out his watch.)*

COUNT: The day is advancing more slowly than I thought. She usually appears at the window much later than this. Never mind; it is better to be too early than to miss that moment of seeing her. If one of my friends at the court guessed that I was a hundred leagues away from Madrid and spending my mornings under the windows of a woman I have never spoken to, he would take me for a romantic of Queen Isabella's time.[1] Well, why not? Every man pursues his own happiness. Mine is in the heart of Rosine. But why follow a woman as far as Seville, when Madrid and the court offer such a selection of easy pleasures? Ah, that is exactly why I ran away. I am bored with these unending conquests of women whose motives are self-interest, social climbing, or vanity. It is sweet to be loved for oneself. And if I could be sure that this disguise—damn, an intruder.

*(*FIGARO *comes in, wearing a guitar, attached bandolier-fashion by a wide ribbon. He has a pencil and paper in his hand.)*

FIGARO *(singing)*:

> Let us not pine.
> It eats us alive.
> But the fire of a good wine
> Helps us revive.
> Without wine, a man
> Is a meaningless loon.

[1] Late fifteenth century. Isabella the Catholic lived from 1451 to 1504. She sponsored Columbus' voyage in 1492.

21

> He lives out a gray span
> And dies off too soon.

That's not bad. Up to now. What next?

> And dies off too soon . . .
> Yes, good wine and idleness
> Fight for my heart . . .

No, they don't fight, they rule there together, peacefully:

> *Reign* in my heart.

Can you say "reign"? I don't see why not. When you're writing a comic opera, you can't stop to look at every word. Nowadays, if a thing isn't worth saying, you sing it.

> Yes, good wine and idleness
> Reign in my heart. . . .

I'd like to end with something beautiful, brilliant, glittering, something with a kick in it. (*He goes down on one knee and writes as he sings.*)

> Reign in my heart.
> If one takes my tenderness,
> The other gives me happiness.

No, no. That's flat. That's not it. I need a clash, an antithesis:

> If one is my mistress
> The other . . .

Yes, perfect:

> The other's my tart.

Well done, Figaro. (*He writes as he sings.*)

> Yes, good wine and idleness
> Reign in my heart.
> If one is my mistress,
> The other's my tart.
> The other's my tart.
> The other's my tart.

Just wait until there's an orchestra behind it, and I'll show you critics if I don't know what I'm talking about. (*He sees the* COUNT.) I've seen that reverend somewhere before. (*He stands up.*)

COUNT (*aside*):   I'm sure I know that man.

FIGARO: No, he isn't a reverend. That haughtiness, that nobility . . .

COUNT: That grotesque shape . . .

FIGARO: I wasn't wrong: it's Count Almaviva.

COUNT: I believe it's that rogue Figaro.

FIGARO: It certainly is, my lord.

COUNT: Fool, if you say one word . . .

FIGARO: It's you all right, my lord. I recognized you. You always honored me with that kind of friendly greeting.

COUNT: I can't say I recognized you. Look how fat and flabby you are. . . .

FIGARO: What do you expect, sir? That's poverty for you.

COUNT: Poor creature. What are you doing in Seville? I gave you references for a job with the government.

FIGARO: I took that job, and don't think I'm not grateful, my lord.

COUNT: Call me Lindor. Can't you see by my disguise that I don't want to be known?

FIGARO: I'll go away.

COUNT: No, stay here. I am waiting for something, and two men standing and talking look less suspicious than one walking about on his own. So pretend we're talking. Now, about the job . . .

FIGARO: The minister took Your Excellency's recommendation into account and, without hesitation, made me assistant medicine-mixer.

COUNT: For all army hospitals?

FIGARO: No, for all the royal stud farms in Andalusia.

COUNT (*laughing*):   A fine beginning.

FIGARO: It wasn't bad. I was in charge of bandages and drugs, and I often sold good horse medicine to men. . . .

COUNT: Which killed the king's subjects.

FIGARO: Ah, there's no universal remedy. But sometimes they got over it. They're tough people in Galicia, Catalonia, and Auvergnat.

COUNT: Why did you give it up?

FIGARO: It gave me up. Someone told the government what I was up to:

"Crooked-fingered Envy, with pale and livid hue . . ."

COUNT: Spare me that. Do you write poetry too? I saw

you kneeling and scribbling and singing over there before.

FIGARO: That was exactly my trouble. When someone reported to the minister that I was composing bouquets of verse—and rather well, if I say so myself—dedicated to Chloris,[2] and that I was sending puzzles and madrigals to the newspapers, and then when he learned that I was suddenly in print, he took a dim view of it and made me give up my job, on the pretext that literature and business don't go together.

COUNT: Good reasoning. But couldn't you make him understand?

FIGARO: I thought it was better for him to forget about me. A great man is doing you enough good when he isn't doing you harm.

COUNT: You're not telling me everything. When you were in my employ, you were a pretty slovenly character.

FIGARO: Well, my lord, you can't expect a poor man to be perfect.

COUNT: Lazy, disorganized . . .

FIGARO: A servant is expected to be as virtuous as his master, my lord, but do you know many masters who are fit to be good servants?

COUNT (*laughing*):   A sharp point. And so you retired to this city?

FIGARO: No, not straight away.

COUNT (*stopping him*):   One moment. I thought she was . . . Keep talking. I am still listening.

FIGARO: Back in Madrid, I thought I'd try my literary talents out again, and the theater seemed to be the most likely field of honor. . . .

COUNT: God save us!

FIGARO (*during this speech, the* COUNT *watches the blind of* ROSINE's *window*):   I can't think why I wasn't the greatest success; I filled the orchestra with solid supporters; they had hands like washboards. I insisted: no gloves or canes—nothing that might deaden the applause—and, on my honor, before the opening, everyone in the café across the street [3] seemed to be on my side. But the critics turned up in force. . . .

COUNT: Ah, the critics. And the author's preparations were undermined?

---

[2] Generic name for short poems addressed to a lady on her birthday, wedding, etc.

[3] A dig at the café opposite the Comédie-Française.

FIGARO: It can happen to anybody. They booed me. But if ever I get that audience together again . . .

COUNT: You'll have your revenge by boring them to death?

FIGARO: I'll have my revenge. I'm saving it for them, by Christ.

COUNT: Are you still angry enough to swear about it? In the Palace of Justice, you know, you have only twenty-four hours to curse your judges.

FIGARO: In the theater you have twenty-four years; a lifetime is too short to get over my kind of resentment.

COUNT: It's good to see how you enjoy your anger. But you haven't told me what made you leave Madrid.

FIGARO: Must have been my good angel, sir, since I've been lucky enough to find my old master again. I saw that the men of letters in Madrid were a pack of wolves, always attacking each other. Authors were beset by their cousins, their critics, their booksellers, their censors, the people who envied them and the people who imitated them—all these insects, these mosquitoes, fastened themselves to the skin of the unfortunate authors and sucked them dry. And so I left Madrid, tired of writing, bored with myself, disgusted with other people; my debts heavy and my pockets light; convinced once and for all that the useful income from a razor is better than the doubtful honors of a pen. I took my baggage on my back and traveled philosophically through the two Castiles, La Mancha, Estremadura, Sierra Morena, and Andalusia, being acclaimed in one town, jailed in another, but always on top of events; praised by these people, denounced by those people; helping out in good times, making do in bad times, taunting all the fools and daunting all the knaves; laughing at my misfortune and clipping every beard I came across. And here I am at last in Seville, where you see me ready to serve Your Excellency in whatever capacity you desire.

COUNT: Who gave you such a joyful philosophy?

FIGARO: Lady Misfortune. I force myself to laugh at everything for fear of being forced to weep at it. What do you keep looking at over there?

COUNT: Let's get away.

FIGARO: Why?

COUNT: Come on, dolt. You'll ruin my plans.

(*They go out. The blind on the first floor of the house is pulled back and* BARTHOLO *and* ROSINE *appear at the window.*)

ROSINE: How delightful to breathe this fresh air! The window is so rarely open.

BARTHOLO: What is that paper you are holding?

ROSINE: Some verses from *The Useless Precaution,* which my singing teacher gave me yesterday.

BARTHOLO: What is *The Useless Precaution?*

ROSINE: It's a new comedy.

BARTHOLO: Another play, eh? More of this modern rubbish? [4]

ROSINE: I don't know.

BARTHOLO: The newspapers and the government are to blame. This is a barbarous century!

ROSINE: You're always abusing our poor century.

BARTHOLO: Pardon the liberty. What has it produced that it should be praised? Every kind of stupidity: freedom of thought, the law of gravity, electricity, religious tolerance, inoculation, quinine, the encyclopedia—and plays that anybody can understand. . . .

(*The paper falls out of* ROSINE's *hands, into the street.*)

ROSINE: Oh, dear. My song! My song fell while I was listening to you. Hurry down after it, sir, hurry; it will blow away.

BARTHOLO: When you're holding something, hold on to it. (*He leaves the balcony.*)

ROSINE (*looks back inside and hisses into the street*): Psst, psst. (*The* COUNT *appears.*) Pick up the paper, quickly, and hide. (*The* COUNT *bounds forward, picks up the paper, and goes off.*)

BARTHOLO (*coming out of the house and looking about*): Where is it? I can't see anything.

ROSINE: Under the balcony, at the foot of the wall.

BARTHOLO: I can't see a thing. Did anybody else pass by?

ROSINE: Not that I saw.

BARTHOLO (*to himself*): And I'm soft enough to look for it. Bartholo, you're an indulgent old fool. This will teach you never to open street windows. (*He goes in again.*)

ROSINE (*still on the balcony*): My plight has driven me to do this: I am alone, trapped, and persecuted by an objectionable man. Is it a crime to escape from slavery?

BARTHOLO (*coming on to the balcony*): Come inside, young lady. I am to blame if your song is lost; it was bad

───────────

4 Bartholo did not like plays. Perhaps in his youth he had written some tragedy. . . . [Note by Beaumarchais.]

luck but it won't happen again, I promise you. (*He locks the window with a key.*)

(*The* COUNT *and* FIGARO *re-enter cautiously.*)

COUNT: Now that they've gone inside, let's look at this song, which must contain some hidden message. It is a letter.

FIGARO: He asked what *The Useless Precaution* was!

COUNT (*reading eagerly*):   "I am curious to know why you are interested in me. As soon as my guardian goes out, sing the tune to these verses, casually, and let me know the name, the rank, and the intentions of the man who seems to be so obstinately concerned with the unfortunate Rosine."

FIGARO (*imitating* ROSINE's *voice*):   Oh, dear. My song! My song fell. Hurry down after it, sir, hurry! (*He laughs.*) These women! Do you want to make the most innocent one deceitful? Then lock her up.

COUNT: My dear Rosine!

FIGARO: Now I understand why you are wearing that disguise, my lord; you're planning to court her.

COUNT: Correct. But if you tattle . . .

FIGARO: Figaro tattle? My lord, I'm not going to pour out those highfalutin phrases about honor and devotion to reassure you; people break them every day. All I want to say is: my self-interest is in your hands; weigh it, balance it, and . . .

COUNT: Good enough. You may as well know that six months ago, on the Prado,[5] I happened to meet a young woman of such beauty—well, you have just seen her. I sent throughout Madrid to find her. No luck. A few days ago I discovered that she is called Rosine, that she is an orphan of noble blood, and that she is married to an old doctor of this city named Bartholo.

FIGARO: A pretty little bird. Not easy to dislodge from the nest. But who told you she was the doctor's wife?

COUNT: Everybody.

FIGARO: That's a story he invented when he got back from Madrid to mislead the young men of Seville and keep them away. She is still only his ward. But before long . . .

COUNT (*spiritedly*):   Never! Not after that piece of news! I'd made up my mind to risk everything just to apologize to her—and I find she's free. There isn't a moment to lose. I must get her to love me, and then I must snatch her away from him. How well do you know this guardian?

[5] **One** of the principal streets of Madrid.

FIGARO: Like my own mother.

COUNT: What kind of a man is he?

FIGARO: A fine, fat, short, young old man, going gray, sly, spry, and secretive, who pries and spies and grumbles and groans, all at the same time.

COUNT (*impatiently*):   Yes, I have seen him. But his character?

FIGARO: Brutal, miserly, loving, and excessively jealous of his ward, who hates him like death.

COUNT: Then how can he please her?

FIGARO: He can't.

COUNT: Even better. Is he honest?

FIGARO: Just enough to keep him this side of the gallows.

COUNT: Better still. I'll punish a rascal while I'm rewarding myself.

FIGARO: Then you'll serve the public and private welfare at the same time. Truly, sir, a masterpiece of morality.

COUNT: You say he locks his door because he's afraid of young men?

FIGARO: Of everybody. If he could, he'd make the place airtight.

COUNT: That's not so good. Do you have any way of getting in?

FIGARO: Haven't I just: First, the house I live in belongs to the doctor, who lets me stay there gratis.

COUNT: Aha!

FIGARO: Yes. And I agree, in return, to pay him a rent of six gold coins a year, also gratis.

COUNT (*impatiently*):   But you're his tenant?

FIGARO: That's not all: I'm his barber, his surgeon, and his apothecary. Every razor, lancet, and syringe in his house is wielded by the hand of yours truly.

COUNT (*embracing him*):   Figaro, you are my friend, my guardian angel, my liberator, my savior.

FIGARO: I see. Now I'm useful to you we're close friends. Talk about passion . . .

COUNT: Lucky Figaro. You are going into that house to see my Rosine, to *see* her. Do you realize how lucky you are?

FIGARO: A typical lover's remark. Am *I* in love with her? I only wish you could take my place.

COUNT: If we could get past the servants who are watching . . .

FIGARO: That's what I was thinking.

COUNT: Just for twelve hours.

FIGARO: Keep servants busy with their own affairs and they don't interfere with other people's.
COUNT: I agree. What about it?
FIGARO: The pharmacy . . . I've just thought of a harmless way to keep them quiet. . . .
COUNT: Villain!
FIGARO: I'm not going to hurt them, am I? They all need my drugs. It's only a question of treating them all at the same time.
COUNT: But the doctor may become suspicious.
FIGARO: We must work so fast that the suspicion will never be born. I have an idea: the regiment of the Royal Infanta is coming into town.
COUNT: The colonel is a friend of mine.
FIGARO: Good. Get hold of a cavalryman's uniform and present yourself at the doctor's house with a billeting order. He'll have to put you up. Leave everything else to me.
COUNT: Excellent.
FIGARO: It might be good if you looked a bit sozzled.
COUNT: Why?
FIGARO: And be impudent with him.
COUNT: Why?
FIGARO: So that he doesn't get wind of anything. He'll think you're more anxious to sleep than to plot in his house.
COUNT: Good idea. What will you be doing?
FIGARO: Never mind me. We'll be lucky if he doesn't recognize you; still, he's never seen you. How are you going to introduce yourself?
COUNT: That will be tricky.
FIGARO: It may be too hard a part for you to play. A cavalryman, and drunk . . .
COUNT: Are you serious? Listen to this. (*In a drunken tone.*) Is this the residence of Doctor Bartholo?
FIGARO: Not bad at all. But a little more intoxication around the knees. (*In a drunker tone.*) Is this the residence of Doctor Bartholo?
COUNT: No, that's how commoners get drunk.
FIGARO: The best way. And the most enjoyable.
COUNT: The door is opening.
FIGARO: That's our man. Let's keep out of the way till he's gone.

(*They hide.* BARTHOLO *comes out of the house.*)

BARTHOLO (*looking inside*): I'll be right back. Don't let anybody in. (*To himself.*) I was stupid to have come down.

The moment she asked me I should have stopped and thought. . . . And Bazile still hasn't come. He is supposed to make all arrangements for the secret marriage tomorrow; and not a word from him. I'll go and see what's holding him up. (*Exit.*)

COUNT: What was that? He's marrying Rosine in secret, tomorrow?

FIGARO: The harder it is to succeed, sir, the more necessary it is to try.

COUNT: Who is this Bazile who is involved in the marriage?

FIGARO: A poor devil who teaches the young lady music; in love with his art, a petty swindler, so out of money that he'll go down on his knees for the smallest coin, and no trouble at all for us to deal with, my lord. (*Looking up at the window.*) There she is, there she is.

COUNT: There who is?

FIGARO: Behind her blind, up there, up there! Don't look, though, don't look.

COUNT: Why not?

FIGARO: Remember what she wrote: "Sing the verses casually." In other words, sing as if you were singing to yourself, just for the sake of singing. Ah, there she is again.

COUNT: Since she's already interested in me without knowing who I am, I'll keep this name Lindor; it'll be better to hide my title until I've won her. (*He unfolds the paper that* ROSINE *dropped.*) But what can I sing to this music? I can't just make up lines.

FIGARO: Yes you can. Sing whatever comes to you. In love the heart assists the mind. Take my guitar.

COUNT: What do I do? I hardly know how to hold it.

FIGARO: Is there actually something a man like you doesn't know? With the back of your fingers: strum, strum, strum. . . . You can't sing without a guitar in Seville. You'll be recognized and rooted out in no time. I'll be here, if you need any help.

(*He goes close to the wall, below the balcony. The* COUNT *sings and walks about, accompanying himself on the guitar.*)

COUNT:

> You ask me to give you my name,
> But, unknown, I dared to adore you.
> After naming myself I implore you
> To allow me to love you the same.

FIGARO (*low*):   It's going well. Keep it up.
COUNT:

> I am Lindor, a man of low birth,
> My pledge is a simple, sincere one:
> I wish I could offer my dear one
> High rank and estates of great worth.

FIGARO: I'll be damned. I couldn't do better myself, and this is my vocation.
COUNT:

> I'll tenderly sing of my love,
> My love that is not yet requited,
> I'll think of you and be excited
> To know you are listening above.

FIGARO: For that verse you deserve—(*Kisses the hem of the* COUNT'*s cloak.*)
COUNT: Figaro.
FIGARO: Your Excellency?
COUNT: Do you think she heard me?
ROSINE (*singing inside*):

> Everything tells me that Lindor is charming
> And that I must love him constantly . . .

(*A window slams. The singing stops.*)

FIGARO: Now do you think she heard you?
COUNT: She closed her window. Evidently someone came into her room.
FIGARO: Poor child! Her voice was shaking. She is yours, my lord.
COUNT: She was singing to a melody from *The Useless Precaution*, too. "Everything tells me that Lindor is charming." What style! What perception!
FIGARO: What dishonesty! What love!
COUNT: Figaro, do you think she'll give in to me?
FIGARO: She won't give you up. She'd rather leap out of that window.
COUNT: It's settled. I belong to Rosine . . . for life.
FIGARO: You forget, my lord, that she can't hear you now.
COUNT: One more thing, Figaro: she is going to be my wife; and if you serve me well and don't tell her my

name . . . well, you understand me, you know me. . . .

FIGARO: I'm on your side, all of me. Come, Figaro, fly toward fortune, my boy.

COUNT: We'd better move away, before anyone becomes inquisitive.

FIGARO: My lord, I shall enter this house and, with the aid of my black arts, I shall wave my wand once and put vigilance to sleep and bring love awake, battle jealousy, baffle intrigue, and overturn all obstacles. You, sir, must go to my house and wait there in soldier's uniform, with a billeting order and gold in your pockets.

COUNT: Gold? For whom?

FIGARO: Gold. Just gold, that's all; gold is the sinews of intrigue.

COUNT: Say no more, Figaro. I'll bring a pile of it.

FIGARO (*moving away*): I'll join you shortly.

COUNT: Figaro!

FIGARO: What?

COUNT: Your guitar.

FIGARO (*coming back*): Forgetting my precious guitar, me! I'm losing my mind. (*Takes it and goes.*)

COUNT (*calling after him*): Where's your house, numskull?

FIGARO (*coming back*): Amnesia, it's caught up with me at last. My shop is a few steps away from here, my lord; it's painted blue with lead window frames, three basins in the air,[6] the eye in the hand, and a big sign over the door: "Figaro." (*Rushes off.*)

---

[6] The insignia of the barber surgeon in France; the three bowls were to catch the blood of patients during "bleedings." The other sign, the "eye in the hand," was to indicate the barber's dexterity, as though his hands could see where they were going.

ACT II

(ROSINE's *quarters in* BARTHOLO's *house. The window at the rear is closed by a grilled ironwork shutter.* ROSINE *is alone at a table with a lighted candle in a candlestick. She takes some paper and writes on it.*)

ROSINE: Marceline is sick; all the men are busy; and nobody will see me writing. I don't know if these walls have ears and eyes or if my Argus has an evil spirit that reports back to him, but I cannot say a word or take a step that he doesn't know about immediately. Ah, Lindor. (*She closes the letter.*) I'll seal this letter, although I don't know when or how I'll be able to give it to him. I saw him through my window, talking to the barber Figaro for a long time. I like Figaro; he has often shown pity for me; if only I had a chance to speak to him. (FIGARO *comes in.*) Mr. Figaro, I am glad to see you.

FIGARO: Aren't you well, madam?

ROSINE: Not too well, Mr. Figaro. I'm dying of boredom.

FIGARO: I believe you. Only fools thrive on it.

ROSINE: You were chatting away to somebody outside. I couldn't hear what you were saying, but . . .

FIGARO: A relative of mine, a very promising young fellow, full of wit, imagination, and talent, and very good-looking.

ROSINE: Yes, I can imagine that. What is his name?

FIGARO: Lindor. He has no money, but if he hadn't left Madrid suddenly he could have found a good job there.

ROSINE: He will find one somewhere else, Mr. Figaro. A young man of that description will make his mark.

FIGARO (*aside*): Good, good. (*Aloud.*) But he has one great weakness, which may work against him.

ROSINE: A weakness, Mr. Figaro? A weakness, are you sure?

FIGARO: He is in love.

ROSINE: In love—and you call that a weakness?

33

FIGARO: Well, only in relation to his lack of money.

ROSINE: Fate is unkind. And has he told you whom he loves? I'm just curious. . . .

FIGARO: Madam, you are the last person I can talk to about this.

ROSINE (*quickly*): Why, Mr. Figaro? I am discreet. This young man is your relative and I am very interested in him. Do tell me who she is.

FIGARO (*watching her cunningly*): Imagine the prettiest little darling, sweet, tender, fresh, delightful and appetizing, light-footed and slender-figured with plump arms and rosebud lips—and hands!—and cheeks!—and teeth!—and eyes!

ROSINE: Does she live in this city?

FIGARO: In this part of it.

ROSINE: In this street, by chance?

FIGARO: Two paces away from me.

ROSINE: How convenient . . . for your relative. And this person is . . . ?

FIGARO: Haven't I as good as told you her name?

ROSINE: That is the one thing you forgot, Mr. Figaro. So tell me, tell me quickly; if someone comes in I won't know.

FIGARO: Do you insist, madam? Well then, she is . . . the ward of your guardian.

ROSINE: The ward . . . ?

FIGARO: Of Doctor Bartholo, yes, madam.

ROSINE (*with emotion*): Ah, Mr. Figaro, I don't believe you.

FIGARO: And he is burning to come here and talk to you himself.

ROSINE: You make me nervous, Mr. Figaro.

FIGARO: It's no good being nervous. Once you give in to the fear of evil, you begin to feel the evil of fear. Besides, I have just got rid of all your guards until tomorrow.

ROSINE: If he loves me, he should prove it by remaining absolutely quiet about it.

FIGARO: Now, now, madam. Can love and peace live in the same heart? Youth is unhappy because it is faced with this terrible choice: love without peace, or peace without love.

ROSINE (*lowering her eyes*): Peace without love . . . seems . . .

FIGARO: Very dull. Love without peace is a lot more exciting; and frankly, if I were a woman . . .

ROSINE (*embarrassed*): Certainly, a young lady cannot prevent a young man from admiring her.

FIGARO: And my relative admires you enormously.
ROSINE: But if he did something rash, Mr. Figaro, we'd
be lost.   .
FIGARO (*aside*):   We would, too. (*Aloud.*) Why don't you
forbid him to? Send him a note. A note is powerful.
ROSINE (*giving him the letter she has just written*):   I
haven't time to rewrite this, but tell him about it . . . be
sure to tell him . . . (*She listens.*)
FIGARO: Nobody there.
ROSINE: . . . that I am doing it out of pure friendship.
FIGARO: Why not say "love"? Love is much more open.
ROSINE: No, out of pure friendship, understand that. I'm
afraid of all the complications. . . .
FIGARO: You think he may turn out to be a will o' the
wisp. But remember, madam: the wind that carries a will o'
the wisp can make a bonfire blaze and that bonfire is the
human heart. When he talks about you he breathes out so
much heat that he almost scorches me. And I'm an outsider.
ROSINE: Hush, I hear my guardian. If he finds you here
. . . Hide in that closet with the harp, and make your way
downstairs, quietly, as soon as you can.
FIGARO: Keep calm. (*Aside, holding up the letter.*) This
is worth all my talk put together. (*Goes into the closet.*)
ROSINE: I'll die of worry until I know he's safely outside.
I like Figaro. He's a fine, honest man, a good relative. Ah,
here comes the tyrant. Back to my embroidery. (*She snuffs
out the candle, sits down, and takes a piece of embroidery
on a frame.*)

(BARTHOLO *storms in.*)

BARTHOLO: Curse him, that mad, vile shark of a Figaro.
A man can't step out of his house for an instant and find
it the same when he gets back. . . .
ROSINE: Who has made you so angry, sir?
BARTHOLO: That damn barber, who has just wrecked my
entire household in one swoop: he gave Lively a sleeping
powder, and Puberty a sneezing powder; he took blood from
Marceline's foot; he even interfered with my mule: he put a
poultice over the eyes of the poor, blind beast. He owes me
a hundred crowns and he'll do anything to cancel out the
debt. But wait till he brings me his bills. And look—nobody
in the antechamber. The house is as empty as a barrack
square and completely unprotected.
ROSINE: Nobody can come in except you, sir.
BARTHOLO: I would rather worry without need than live

without heed. The world is full of swindlers and pirates. Didn't one of them snatch your song this morning, while, I was going down to get it?

ROSINE: You're making a fuss about nothing. The paper may have been picked up by the wind or by a passer-by. How do I know?

BARTHOLO: It was nothing whatever to do with the wind or with a passer-by. It's strange but whenever a woman seems to drop papers by accident someone is always waiting to pick them up.

ROSINE: *Seems*, sir?

BARTHOLO: Yes, *seems*, madam.

ROSINE (*aside*): What a nasty old man.

BARTHOLO: But that's the last time it will happen. I am going to lock the grille.

ROSINE: Don't stop at that: wall up the windows. There's not much difference between a prison and a dungeon.

BARTHOLO: Yes, the windows that open onto the street— not a bad idea. That barber didn't come in to see you, did he?

ROSINE: Are you worried about him too?

BARTHOLO: I worry about everybody.

ROSINE: You answer so politely.

BARTHOLO: Trust the whole world and you'll soon find yourself with a good wife who deceives you, good friends who seduce her, and good servants who assist them.

ROSINE: Don't you even admit that a person could have scruples about letting herself be seduced by a man like Figaro?

BARTHOLO: Who the devil understands women and their scruples?

ROSINE: If it takes a man to please a woman, sir, how is it that you displease me?

BARTHOLO: How—? What do you mean? . . . You still haven't answered my question about the barber.

ROSINE (*furiously*): Then I will. Yes, he did come in here. I did see him. I did speak to him. And I found him very pleasant. And may you die of rage from knowing it. (*Exit.*)

BARTHOLO: Where are you, you dogs, you servants, you bribe-takers? Puberty! Lively, Lively, curses on you both!

(LIVELY *comes in yawning, almost asleep.*)

LIVELY: I—ah, aah, er, ah.

BARTHOLO: Where were you when the barber came in, you plaguey nincompoop?

LIVELY: Sir, I was ah . . . aah, ah . . .

BARTHOLO: Up to some trickery, I bet. Didn't you see him?

LIVELY: I certainly did; from what he said I was quite ill, and he must have been right because I began to ache all over as soon as he told me. Ah, aah, ah . . .

BARTHOLO (*imitating him*): Aah, ah! As soon as he told me . . . Where is that no-good Puberty? How dare he drug a youngster like you without consulting me about the prescription! There's some knavery going on behind my back.

(*Enter* PUBERTY, *an old man on a crutch. He sneezes several times.*)

LIVELY (*still yawning*): Puberty? Is that you?

BARTHOLO: Stop that sneezing on my time. Save it till your day off.

PUBERTY: That makes fifty . . . fifty times in the last minute. (*He sneezes.*) I'm a wreck.

BARTHOLO: Now, listen: I asked you both if anyone came into Rosine's room, and you didn't tell me that this barber . . .

LIVELY: Is Figaro "anyone"? Eh? I . . . ah . . .

BARTHOLO: I bet this scoundrel is in cahoots with him.

LIVELY (*crying like a drunk*): Me, sir, in cahoots . . . ?

PUBERTY (*sneezing*): But, sir, is there no . . . is there no justice?

BARTHOLO: Justice is for dregs, like you, to argue about. I'm the master here and what I say goes.

PUBERTY (*sneezing*): But cripes, right is right. . . .

BARTHOLO: Only when I say so. If idiots like you were ever allowed to be right, what would become of discipline?

PUBERTY (*sneezing*): I'm giving notice. This is a terrible job; it's like being in hell.

LIVELY (*sobbing*): A poor, honest man is called a dreg.

BARTHOLO: Get out, then, you poor, honest man. (*He imitates their sneezes and yawns.*) With your aah's and your tchoo's, yawning and sneezing in my face. (LIVELY *goes out, weeping still.*)

PUBERTY: I swear to you, sir, that it would be impossible to stay in this house if it weren't for Miss Rosine. (*Exit, sneezing.*)

BARTHOLO: What a state that Figaro has got them into! I can see what the thief is up to: he thinks that by administering expensive drugs he's found a way to pay back my hundred crowns without opening his wallet.

(*Enter* DON BAZILE. FIGARO, *who is still hidden in the closet, looks out and listens from time to time.*)

BARTHOLO: Ah, Don Bazile, you've come to give Rosine her music lesson.
BAZILE: That's not important at the moment.
BARTHOLO: I stopped at your house, but you were not in.
BAZILE: I'd gone out to check something for you. And I heard some rather upsetting news.
BARTHOLO: For you?
BAZILE: No, for you. Count Almaviva is here in Seville.
BARTHOLO: Talk quietly. The man who was looking all over Madrid for Rosine?
BAZILE: Yes. He's staying in the Square, and he goes out every day in disguise.
BARTHOLO: This may be serious. What can I do?
BAZILE: We could soon frighten him away if he were an ordinary citizen.
BARTHOLO: Yes. Ambush him one evening; we'd be armed and protected. . . .
BAZILE: *Bone deus!* I know! Why not start a scandal about him? Get a few rumors going and once they're started, add to them. Watch them grow.
BARTHOLO: A curious way to get rid of a man.
BAZILE: Slander, sir, defamation! Don't belittle it. I've seen it destroy the most honest men. Believe me, there's no flat lie, no horror, no absurdity that the scandalmongers in a big city won't gulp down if you tell it right. And the people here gulp like nobody's business. You start with a faint rumor, skimming the earth like a swallow before a storm, *pianissimo,* a murmur, a melody, gently spreading its poison. Somebody passes it on and *piano, piano,* it slips cunningly in and out of ears. The harm is done, but it mounts, it blossoms, and passes in ringing chords *rinforzando* from mouth to mouth at Satan's own speed. Then suddenly—who knows how?—you see Slander rear up, hiss, swell, and grow into a monstrous hurricane before your eyes. And it flings itself about, whirls and reaches out and crushes, plucks up and pulls down, flashes lightning and booms thunder, and becomes, heaven be praised, a general shout, a public *crescendo,* a universal *chorus* of hate and condemnation. Who could stand up to that?
BARTHOLO: What's all this nonsense, Bazile? And how is this *piano-crescendo* business supposed to help me?
BAZILE: That is how people defeat their enemies. This

is how you can defeat *your* enemy before he has a chance to get near you.

BARTHOLO: But I intend to marry Rosine before she even learns that this count exists.

BAZILE: In that case, let's not waste any more time.

BARTHOLO: What's delaying us? I made you responsible for all the details.

BAZILE: Yes, but you've been tight on expenses; when you have dissonances, such as an unequal marriage, an unfair relationship, a gross injustice, you must bring them into harmony by means of gold.

BARTHOLO (*giving him money*):   Take as much as you need. Now let's get on with it.

BAZILE: That's what I like to hear. Tomorrow, everything will be arranged. It's up to you to see that nobody tells Rosine anything today.

BARTHOLO: Trust me. Will you come back this evening, Bazile?

BAZILE: Don't bank on it. Organizing your marriage will keep me busy all day; don't bank on it.

BARTHOLO (*going with him*):   Allow me.

BAZILE: Don't bother, Doctor, don't bother. I can find my way out.

BARTHOLO: It's not that. I want to make sure the front door is closed behind you. (*They go out.*)

(FIGARO *reappears.*)

FIGARO: Oh, these precautions! Yes, close the front door, close it, and when I go out I'll open it again for the count. This Bazile is a crafty scoundrel. Luckily, he's even more of a fool. You need an estate, a family, a name, a rank, in other words, quality, if you want to become a professional scandalmonger. But a Bazile! Oh, no. He'll start inventing stories and nobody will believe him.

(ROSINE *comes running in.*)

ROSINE: What—are you still here, Mr. Figaro?

FIGARO: Luckily for you, madam. Your guardian and your singing teacher thought they were alone, and talked openly. . . .

ROSINE: And you listened to them? You know, that was very naughty.

FIGARO: To listen? But that is the only way to hear prop-

erly. And here's what I heard: your guardian is making arrangements to marry you tomorrow.

ROSINE: How frightening!

FIGARO: Don't be frightened. We'll keep him so busy
that he won't have time to think about it.

ROSINE: He's coming back. Go out down the little stair-
case. You're making me die of fright.

(FIGARO *hastens out. Re-enter* BARTHOLO.)

ROSINE: Was somebody here with you, sir?

BARTHOLO: Don Bazile; I've just seen him out. You can't
be too careful. You'd have been happier if it was Figaro, eh?

ROSINE: It makes no difference to me.

BARTHOLO: I'd like to know what the barber had to say
to you that was so important.

ROSINE: Shall I tell you the truth? He gave me a report
on Marceline's health, and from what he says she isn't too
well.

BARTHOLO: He gave you a report! I'll bet he came to deliver a letter.

ROSINE: From whom? Please tell me.

BARTHOLO: Oh, from . . . from someone that women
never admit they know. How do I know? It may have been
a reply to the paper that fell from the window.

ROSINE (*aside*):   He hasn't missed a thing. (*Aloud.*) If so,
it would serve you right.

BARTHOLO: If so? It *is* so. After all, you have been writing.

ROSINE (*embarrassed*):   It will be interesting if you
can prove that.

BARTHOLO (*taking her right hand*):   I don't need to. See,
your finger still has an ink stain on it. Aha, you cunning girl.

ROSINE (*aside*):   You repulsive old creature.

BARTHOLO (*still holding her hand*):   A woman thinks she's
safe just because she's alone.

ROSINE: That may be, but you haven't proved anything.
Let go, sir, you're twisting my arm. It so happens that I
burnt myself when I was sewing next to this candle, and I've
always heard that it's best to dip a burn in ink. So that's what
I did.

BARTHOLO: So that's what you did? Let's see if we can
find a second piece of evidence to confirm the first. Here's
the notebook; there were six sheets in it; I count them every
morning, and I didn't forget this morning.

ROSINE (*aside*):   I'm a fool—

BARTHOLO (*counting*): Three, four, five . . . (*He looks up.*)

ROSINE: The sixth one . . .

BARTHOLO: Yes, I notice that the sixth one is missing.

ROSINE: I used it to make a cone for some candies I gave Figaro for his little girl.[7]

BARTHOLO: Indeed? And this pen nib, which was new— how did it become dirty? When you were addressing the candy cone to Figaro's little girl?

ROSINE (*aside*): Jealousy is this man's first instinct. (*Aloud.*) I used it for redrawing a faded flower on the jacket I'm embroidering for you.

BARTHOLO: How nice! If you want to be believed, my girl, you mustn't blush as you tell one lie after another. You haven't learned that yet.

ROSINE: Who wouldn't blush, sir, to see you drawing such false conclusions from such innocent behavior?

BARTHOLO: Yes, I must be wrong. You burnt your finger, you dipped it in the ink; you made a candy cone for Figaro's daughter, and you embroidered my jacket. What could be more innocent? But what could be more guilty than piling up all those lies to conceal one single fact: *I am alone,* you thought; *nobody can see me. I can lie to my heart's content.* But your fingertip is still black, the nib is dirty, the paper is missing. Well, one can't think of everything. But from now on, young lady, whenever I go into town, every door in this house will be double-locked. (*The* COUNT *enters, in cavalry uniform, swaying drunkenly and singing: "Reveille, reveille, time to get up in the morning . . ."*) A soldier? What does he want? Go into your bedroom, girl.

COUNT (*advancing and still humming*): Which one of you ladies is Doctor Barcarolle? (*Aside, to* ROSINE.) I am Lindor.

BARTHOLO: The name is Bartholo.

ROSINE (*aside*): He said he was Lindor.

COUNT: Barkalo, Barmy-o, who cares? What I want to know is, which one of you is it? (*To* ROSINE, *handing her a paper.*) Take this letter.

BARTHOLO: Which one? You can see very well that I'm Bartholo. Rosine, go inside. This man has been drinking.

ROSINE: That's why I'd better stay, sir. You'll be alone with him. Soldiers sometimes behave with more courtesy in front of a woman.

BARTHOLO: Go in, go in. I'm not afraid.

---

[7] Figaro's daughter is not explained by Beaumarchais. In a succeeding play, *The Marriage of Figaro,* he weds Suzanne, a chambermaid.

COUNT: It's all right. I recognized you right away by your description.

BARTHOLO: What's that you're hiding in your pocket?

COUNT: Something I'm hiding in my pocket, so that you can't tell what it is.

BARTHOLO: My description! These people always think they're talking to other soldiers.

COUNT: Do you think it would be so hard to describe you? (*Sings.*)

> Shiny head with a big, bald top.
> Different-colored eyes that glare and pop.
> Creeping walk, like a beaten-up hound.
> Sluggish gray body that slops around.
> Shoulder on the right too high by a foot.
> Wooden complexion, with ingrained soot.
> Nose the shape of an unmade bed.
> Balloonlike legs with lead-heavy tread.
> Squalling tone from a grumbling throat.
> Greedy and destructive and as vicious as a stoat.
> A scraggy old, baggy old, cheap-minded churl. . . .
> In short, sir, of doctors you are the pearl.

BARTHOLO: Do you realize that you've insulted me? Is that what you came for? Get out this instant.

COUNT: Get out? Now is that a nice thing to say? Do you now how to read, Doctor Buffalo?

BARTHOLO: That is an insolent question.

COUNT: Don't let it annoy you. I'm at least as much of a doctor as you are. And between doctors . . .

BARTHOLO: You're what?

COUNT: Yes, didn't I tell you? I'm the regimental horse doctor. That's why they sent me here—to lodge with a colleague.

BARTHOLO: How dare you compare me with a blacksmith!

COUNT (*singing*):

> A simple horse doctor like me can't pretend
> That my art is as highly selective
> As yours is, my dear Hippocratical friend,
> For you can be much more effective:
> With the aid of odd drugs and extortionate fees
> And pills and diverse medications,
> You eliminate not merely pain and disease
> But also your patients.

Is that polite enough for you?

BARTHOLO: It's typical of an ignorant shyster like you to decry the first, the greatest and the most useful of the arts. . . .

COUNT: Certainly the most useful to those who practice it.

BARTHOLO: An art whose successes the sun shines upon.

COUNT: An art whose failures the earth tries to conceal.

BARTHOLO: It's obvious that you are not used to talking to anything but horses.

COUNT: But isn't it well known that a horse doctor always cures his patients without talking to them, whereas a doctor always talks to his patients . . .

BARTHOLO: Without curing them? Is that what you were going to say?

COUNT: You've already said it.

BARTHOLO: Who the devil sent this drunken idiot here?

COUNT: Careful; next you'll be spilling epigrams, you lovable old man.

BARTHOLO: What do you want? What have you come for?

COUNT (*pretending to be angry*): He's trying to make me lose control. What do I want? Can't you see?

(ROSINE *comes running in.*)

ROSINE (*to* COUNT): Please don't lose your temper, Mr. Soldier. (*To* BARTHOLO.) Speak to him nicely. He doesn't know what he's doing or saying.

COUNT: You are right. But he's the one who doesn't know what he's doing or saying. We do, don't we? I'm polite and you're pretty . . . that's enough. I've just decided: from now on I'm not going to deal with anyone in this house but you.

ROSINE: And what can I do for you, Mr. Soldier?

COUNT: A small favor, my dear. I hope I am making myself clear?

ROSINE: I'm following the message. . . .

COUNT (*showing her the letter*): No, take the letter, the letter. (*To* BARTHOLO.) All you have to do, and I say this with the greatest respect, is to give me a bed for the night.

BARTHOLO: Is that all?

COUNT: That is all. Read this love letter that our quartermaster has sent you.

BARTHOLO: Let me see. (*The* COUNT *hides the letter and gives him another paper.*) "Doctor Bartholo will receive, feed, accommodate, and sleep . . ."

COUNT (*leaning over his shoulder*): Sleep is the word . . .

BARTHOLO: "For one night only, the undernamed scholar and member of the horse regiment: Lindor . . ."

ROSINE: It is Lindor; that proves it.

BARTHOLO (*swiftly, to* ROSINE): What was that?

COUNT: Well, was I wrong, Doctor Go-below?

BARTHOLO: This man seems to be out to wound me in every way possible. Go to hell with your Go-belows and Buffaloes and tell your impertinent quartermaster that, since I went to Madrid, I've been exempted from accommodating soldiers.

COUNT (*aside*): That's a blow.

BARTHOLO: Ah, my friend, that sobers you up a little. And now you can clear out without wasting any more time.

COUNT (*aside*): I was afraid of this. (*Aloud.*) If you're exempted from lodging soldiers, you're not exempted from being polite. Before I clear out I want to see your certificate of exemption, even if I can't read it.

BARTHOLO: That's no problem. It's in this desk.

COUNT (*softly, without moving*): My lovely Rosine!

ROSINE: Lindor, I'm so happy to see you.

COUNT: Take this letter.

ROSINE: Not now. He's watching.

COUNT: Take out your handkerchief. I'll drop this. (*Approaches.*)

BARTHOLO: Careful, careful, soldier. I don't like strange men to go near my wife.

COUNT: Oh, she's your wife?

BARTHOLO: What else?

COUNT: I took you for her great-grandfather, paternal, maternal, or eternal. There are at least three generations separating you.

BARTHOLO (*reading a document*): "Upon the good and faithful evidence that has been given us . . ."

COUNT (*knocking the papers to the floor*): I don't have to listen to all that garbage. . . .

BARTHOLO: Do you realize, soldier, that if I call my men I can have you thrown out? And that's what you deserve.

COUNT: Ah, a battle? With pleasure. That's my trade, fighting. (*Takes a pistol from his belt.*) And here's what I use to throw dust in their eyes. Have you ever seen a battle, my dear?

ROSINE: No, and I never want to.

COUNT: Nothing is as much fun as a battle. There (*he pushes* BARTHOLO *back*) is the enemy on one side of the ravine, and here we are on the other. (*Aside.*) Take out your handkerchief. (*He spits on the floor.*) And there is the ravine.

(ROSINE *takes out her handkerchief. He drops the letter between her and him.*)
BARTHOLO (*bending forward*):   Ah!
COUNT (*picking up the letter*):   Stand back. I'm about to teach you the secrets of my trade. Now, there's a cautious woman for you. Isn't that a love letter that fell out of her pocket?
BARTHOLO: Give it to me.
COUNT: Easy, Grandpa. It's not your business. How would you like strange people to pick up your quack prescriptions?
ROSINE (*holding out her hand*):   It's mine. I know what it is. (*She takes the letter and puts it in her pocket.*)
BARTHOLO: Will you get out?
COUNT: Yes, I'll get out. Good-by, Doctor. No hard feelings? I have a small request, my dear man: pray that Death may spare me for a few more campaigns. Life has never been so precious before.
BARTHOLO: Go on, get out. Do you think I have a credit account with Death?
COUNT: Why not? You're a doctor. After all you've done for Death, she shouldn't be able to refuse you anything.

(*He goes out.* BARTHOLO *watches him leave.*)

BARTHOLO: At last. (*Aside.*) Now to get around her.
ROSINE: You must admit, sir, that he's a merry young man. Drunk or not drunk, he's obviously neither foolish nor illiterate.
BARTHOLO: We're lucky to be rid of him, my love. And now, aren't we both curious to read that paper he gave you?
ROSINE: Which paper?
BARTHOLO: The one he pretended to pick up for you.
ROSINE: Oh, the one that fell from my pocket. It's from my cousin, the officer.
BARTHOLO: I have an idea that it fell from his pocket.
ROSINE: No, from mine.
BARTHOLO: Well, it won't hurt to look at it.
ROSINE: I don't remember what I did with it.
BARTHOLO (*pointing to her pocket*):   In there.
ROSINE: I wasn't thinking.
BARTHOLO: Of course, of course. It's something idiotic, you'll see.
ROSINE (*aside*):   I'll have to make him angry. There's no other way to refuse.
BARTHOLO: Give it to me, then, my heart.

ROSINE: Why are you insisting, sir? More suspicions?

BARTHOLO: Why don't you want to show it to me?

ROSINE: I've already told you, sir, that this paper is a letter from my cousin, which you opened yesterday before you gave it to me. And while we're on that subject, I'd like to say that you have no right to take such a liberty.

BARTHOLO: I don't understand.

ROSINE: Do I open your mail? Why should you interfere with mine? If you are jealous, it's insulting; if you are trying to show your authority, it's revolting.

BARTHOLO: What? Revolting? You've never spoken to me like that before.

ROSINE: Just because I haven't protested before, it doesn't mean that you have the right to go on insulting me.

BARTHOLO: What insults are you talking about?

ROSINE: It's unheard of for a person to open another person's mail.

BARTHOLO: Even his wife's?

ROSINE: I'm not your wife yet. And if I were, why should you humiliate your wife? You wouldn't do it to a stranger.

BARTHOLO: You're trying to switch the conversation away from that note which is undoubtedly a letter from some lover. But I am determined to see it.

ROSINE: You will not see it. If you come any nearer, I'll run out of the house and ask the first passer-by to protect me.

BARTHOLO: He'll refuse.

ROSINE: We'll see about that.

BARTHOLO: You think we are in France, where women always get their own way. To close that fantasy out, I'll shut the door.

ROSINE (*as he is going*): Now what can I do? I know— change the two letters around and let him find my cousin's. (*She lets her cousin's letter show out of her pocket.*)

BARTHOLO (*coming back*): Now for the letter.

ROSINE: What right have you to look at it?

BARTHOLO: The unanswerable right—of the stronger.

ROSINE: You'll have to kill me before I give it up.

BARTHOLO (*stamping his foot*): Don't waste time . . . I want it now.

ROSINE (*falling into a chair and pretending to be ill*): This is a disgrace.

BARTHOLO: Give me that letter or face my anger.

ROSINE: I am so unhappy. . . .

BARTHOLO: What's wrong with you?

ROSINE (*muttering*): An unbearable future.

BARTHOLO: Rosine!

ROSINE: I am suffocating.

BARTHOLO: She does look ill.

ROSINE: I'm getting weaker. I am dying.

BARTHOLO (*feels her pulse and says, aside*):   There's the letter. I'll read it, while she doesn't realize what's happening.

ROSINE: Nothing but misery left for me.

BARTHOLO (*aside, still holding her wrist*):   How eager we are to learn what we fear to know.

ROSINE: I am for the grave.

BARTHOLO: It must be her perfume that causes those spasms. (*He reads the letter behind the chair, still feeling her pulse.* ROSINE *raises herself a little, looks at him slyly, nods to herself, and pretends to move restlessly again.*) Oh, God. It *is* her cousin's letter. And I was so worried. How can I calm her down? She mustn't know I've read this. (*Pretends to sit her up, and slips the letter back in her pocket.*)

ROSINE (*sighing*):   Ah . . .

BARTHOLO: Now then, my child, it's nothing at all: the vapors rising inside you to your brain, that's all. Your pulse is normal. (*He takes a medicine bottle from a cabinet.*)

ROSINE (*aside*):   He has put the letter back. Good.

BARTHOLO: Here you are, Rosine dear. A little spirit water.

ROSINE: I don't want anything from you. Leave me.

BARTHOLO: Perhaps I was too forceful about that letter.

ROSINE: It's nothing to do with the letter. It's your way of asking for things that makes me furious.

BARTHOLO (*on his knees*):   Forgive me. I admit I was wrong. Here I am at your feet, ready to make amends.

ROSINE: Forgive you? When you believe this letter is not from my cousin?

BARTHOLO: It makes no difference whether it's from him or somebody else. Don't tell me.

ROSINE (*handing him the letter*):   You see, when you ask me properly you can have anything. Read it.

BARTHOLO: Your honesty has convinced me. I was unkind to suspect you.

ROSINE: Read it anyway.

BARTHOLO (*moving away*):   God forbid that I do you such an injury.

ROSINE: You will annoy me if you refuse.

BARTHOLO: No, let it be my sign of confidence in you. I think I'll go and see how poor Marceline is getting on. Would you like to come?

ROSINE: I'll come up in a moment.

BARTHOLO: Now that we have made up, my dear, give me your hand. Ah, if you could only love me you would be so happy.

ROSINE: If you could only please me, perhaps I could love you.

BARTHOLO: I shall please you, I shall. When I say that, I mean it. (*Goes out.*)

ROSINE: Lindor, he says that he will please me. Now I can read this letter which almost got me into so much trouble. (*She reads and cries out.*) Too late. He advises me to remain on bad terms with my guardian. I had that beautiful quarrel going and now I've patched it up. When he gave me this letter I felt myself blushing to the eyes. My guardian is right: I do give myself away; I haven't the sophistication of a woman of the world. But an unjust man can soon turn an innocent girl into a schemer.

ACT III

(BARTHOLO's *study*.)

BARTHOLO (*alone and sad*): What a temper that girl has! She seems to have calmed down now, but who gave her the idea of not having her piano lesson with Don Bazile? She must have guessed that he is mixed up in this marriage arrangement. (*A knock on the door*.) You do everything you can to please women, but if you forget one tiny thing, just one . . . (*Another knock*.) I'll see who this is.

(*The* COUNT *comes in, dressed as a young scholar, in a jacket, breeches, high socks, priest's cloak, neck ruff*.)

COUNT: Peace and joy on this house forevermore.

BARTHOLO (*shortly*): Nobody ever made a more appropriate wish. What do you want?

COUNT: Sir, I am Alonzo, a licensed instructor . . .

BARTHOLO: I don't need an instructor.

COUNT: . . . of music, the pupil of Don Bazile, organist of the Grand Convent, who has the honor of teaching music to your ward. . . .

BARTHOLO: Yes, I know all that—he's an organist and he has the honor and so on. What about it?

COUNT (*aside*): What a man. (*Aloud*.) A sudden sickness has forced him to take to his bed. . . .

BARTHOLO: To his bed, Bazile! Just as well that he informed me. I'll go and see him at once.

COUNT (*aside*): Damn! (*Aloud*.) When I say he's in bed, sir, I mean that he is staying in his room.

BARTHOLO: Only indisposed? Well, we'll go, anyway. Lead the way; I'll follow you.

COUNT (*embarrassed*): Sir, he asked me to . . . Can anybody hear us?

BARTHOLO (*aside*): Some rascal or other. (*Aloud*.) No, sir. Speak up, don't be mysterious. Talk freely, if you can.

49

COUNT (*aside*):   The old scourge. (*Aloud.*) Don Bazile asked me to tell you . . .

BARTHOLO: Louder. I am deaf in one ear.

COUNT (*raising his voice*):   Certainly. Count Almaviva, who is staying at the Square . . .

BARTHOLO (*nervously*):   Not so loud.

COUNT (*louder*):   . . . left his house this morning. It was through me that Don Bazile discovered that Count Almaviva . . .

BARTHOLO: Quietly, please. *Please!*

COUNT (*just as loudly*):   . . . was in this city, and I have discovered that Miss Rosine has written to him. . . .

BARTHOLO: She has? My dear friend, please don't shout, I beg of you. Why don't we sit down and chat quietly? Now, you say you've discovered that Rosine . . .

COUNT (*noisily*):   That's right. Bazile thought you ought to know about this correspondence and asked me to show you her letter; except that you take things too badly. . . .

BARTHOLO: I do? Don't you worry about the way I take things. But please, please, keep your voice down.

COUNT: You said you're deaf in one ear.

BARTHOLO: I am sorry, Señor Alonzo, if I seemed suspicious and blunt; but I am surrounded by schemers and traps . . . and then your bearing, your age, your manner . . . I'm sorry. So, you have the letter?

COUNT: All in good time, sir, now that you are talking politely. But I am afraid someone may be listening.

BARTHOLO: Who? My servants are all helpless; Rosine has shut herself in her room to sulk. The devil has taken over this house. But I'd better make sure. . . . (*Goes to* ROSINE's *room and opens the door gently.*)

COUNT (*aside*):   I'm hemmed in by spite. Must hold on to the letter for the time being. I shall have to run. Better never to have come than to show it to him. If I can only warn Rosine, though, it will be a master stroke to show it to him. . . .

BARTHOLO (*coming back*):   She's sitting next to the window, with her back to the door, reading that letter from her cousin, which I looked at. Now let's see your letter.

COUNT: Here it is. (*Aside.*) She is reading my letter.

BARTHOLO (*from the letter the* COUNT *has given him*):   "Since you have told me your name and rank . . ." Ah, treachery! It is certainly her handwriting.

COUNT (*nervously*):   Now it's your turn to keep your voice down.

BARTHOLO: What are you planning, my friend?

COUNT: When this is all over, you will be her husband, I assure you. Bazile is making arrangements at this moment with a lawyer. . . .

BARTHOLO: For my marriage?

COUNT: Of course. Why else would I warn you against telling her? He told me to say that everything would be ready tomorrow. Then, if she objects . . .

BARTHOLO: She will.

COUNT (*trying to reclaim the letter;* BARTHOLO *holds on to it*): . . . that's when I can be of service to you. We will show her the letter and, if necessary (*mysteriously*), I'll even tell her that I got it from a woman who had wheedled it away from the count. Do you understand? The shame, the anguish, will make her . . .

BARTHOLO: Ah, slander! Now, my dear boy, I am convinced that you are working for Bazile. But to prevent her from thinking this is a conspiracy, shouldn't she meet you first?

COUNT (*trying not to appear anxious*): That is what Don Bazile thought. But how can we do it? Time is running out. . . .

BARTHOLO: I'll tell her that you are taking his place. You could give her a music lesson, couldn't you?

COUNT: Anything to please you. But take care not to make her think there's a plot against her. Don't be melodramatic. What if she suspects something?

BARTHOLO: She won't. I'll introduce you myself. You look more like a disguised lover than an official friend.

COUNT: Do you think that will help the deception?

BARTHOLO: I'm sure of it. She is in a terrible mood this evening. But as soon as she sees you . . . Her harpsichord is in that closet. You can play it while you're waiting for her. I'll persuade her to come in somehow.

COUNT: Be sure not to mention the letter to her.

BARTHOLO: I won't. Not before the crucial moment. It would lose its effect. You never have to repeat anything to me. No, you never have to repeat anything to me. (*Exit.*)

COUNT: I've done it. What a hard man to handle! Figaro was right about him. I could tell I was lying badly; that made me even more hesitant. And he has eyes like knives. If I hadn't thought of the letter, I swear I'd have been dismissed like an idiot. They're arguing in there. Suppose she won't come out? (*He goes to the door and listens.*) She refuses to meet me. All my efforts have been wasted. No, here she comes. I'd better not show myself at first. (*Hides in the closet.*)

Rosine (*pretending to be angry*): It's useless to talk to me, sir. I have made up my mind. I don't want to hear another word about music.

Bartholo: But listen, my dear, it's Señor Alonzo, the pupil and friend of Don Bazile, and chosen by him to be one of our witnesses. A little music will soothe you.

Rosine: Spare yourself the trouble. If I sing this evening, it will only be because . . . But where is this music teacher that you are afraid of sending away? (*The* Count *comes out of the closet quietly.*) I'll tell him what I think of him and of Don Bazile. (*She sees the* Count.) Oh!

Bartholo: What's wrong?

Rosine: Nothing, nothing.

Bartholo: She is ill again, Señor Alonzo.

Rosine: No, I am not ill. But as I was turning—oh! . . .

Count: You twisted your foot, madam?

Rosine: What? Yes, I twisted my foot. The pain is awful.

Count: I saw you do it.

Rosine (*looking at the* Count): The pain went straight to my heart.

Bartholo: A seat, a seat! There isn't an armchair here. (*Goes for one.*)

Count: Ah, Rosine.

Rosine: You are too rash.

Count: I have a thousand things to tell you.

Rosine: He won't leave us alone.

Count: Figaro will help us.

Bartholo (*bringing in an armchair*): Here you are, my darling, sit down. It doesn't look as if she'll be able to take her music lesson this evening, Señor Alonzo; it'll have to wait. Good night.

Rosine (*to* Count): No, stay. The pain is not so severe now. (*To* Bartholo.) I have been unfair to you, sir. I'd like to make it up to you, by following your good example. . . .

Bartholo: Oh, you sweet, dear little thing. But you have been so upset that I don't want you to strain yourself in the least. Good-by, señor.

Rosine (*to* Count): One moment, please. (*To* Bartholo.) If you stop me from taking my lesson, sir, I shall think that you don't want me to prove how sorry I am.

Count (*quietly, to* Bartholo): Take my advice: don't cross her.

Bartholo: Anything you wish, my love, I am so eager not to displease you, I'll stay here during the whole lesson.

Rosine: No need to, sir. I know that you don't like music.

BARTHOLO: This evening I shall love it.

ROSINE (*aside, to* COUNT): I can't get rid of him.

COUNT (*taking a piece of paper from the desk*): Would you like to sing this, my lady?

ROSINE: Yes, it's a very nice song from *The Useless Precaution.*

BARTHOLO: *The Useless Precaution* again.

COUNT: It's all the rage today. It's a song about spring, a very sweet melody. And, now, if you'd like to try it . . .

ROSINE: With pleasure. I love the idea of spring; the young days of Nature. Winter has disappeared and the heart becomes sensitive, like a slave who has been locked up for a long time and then appreciates his liberty more than ever.

BARTHOLO (*to* COUNT, *quietly*): Her head's still full of romantic ideas.

COUNT (*quietly*): You realize where they can lead?

BARTHOLO: Yes, yes. (*He sits in the armchair he brought in for* ROSINE.)

ROSINE (*sings*):

> When love doth bring
> The first of spring
> To fire the flowers
> And warm the hours
> And overjoy young hearts—
> A bird sings praises
> To the sun
> A new lamb grazes,
> Everyone
> Is glad when springtime starts.

COUNT (*sings*):

> And Lindor dreams in happiness
> Of being loved by his shepherdess.

ROSINE (*sings*):

> For though they may be
> Watched and spied on
> Not knowing who can
> Be relied on—
> This is the test
> That makes love surer,
> Stronger and purer. . . .
> Yes, lovers are deeply impressed:
> The spring of the year is best.

(BARTHOLO *has fallen asleep, and the* COUNT *has been kissing* ROSINE's *hands while she was singing. Now that she has stopped,* BARTHOLO *wakes up. The* COUNT *stands up.* ROSINE *begins to sing the second verse again.* BARTHOLO *is again lulled to sleep. Finally*:)

COUNT: Madam, you sang that with great feeling.

ROSINE: You flatter me, sir. It was your encouragement. . . .

BARTHOLO (*yawning*): I must have dozed off during that charming interlude. What with patients all the time, I have to run here and there, and as soon as I sit down and take the weight off my legs, it's good night again. (*Gets up and pushes the armchair back.*)

ROSINE (*softly, to the* COUNT): Figaro isn't coming.

COUNT: We'll have to spin out the talk.

BARTHOLO: You know, I keep telling old Bazile, there must be something for Rosine to study that's a bit livelier than all these grand arias which go up and down with the trills and the frills and the doh-soh-me-doh-me-soh's. They're like burial marches. Give me those catchy little melodies we used to sing when I was a lad; they were so easy to remember. I used to know them all. For instance . . . (*He scratches his head to help his memory, then sings, snapping his fingers and thumbs and kicking up his knees.*)

> Oh, my pretty Rosinette,
> Will you marry me and get
> The monarch of the merry swains . . .

(*To the* COUNT, *laughing.*) In the original song it was Fanchonette, but I substituted Rosinette to bring it up to date. Ha, ha, ha, ha. Pretty smart, eh?

COUNT (*laughing*): Yes, devastating.

BARTHOLO (*singing*):

> Oh, my pretty Rosinette,
> Will you marry me and get
> The monarch of the merry swains,
> Youth and tenderness and brains?
>
> I may not be handsome, yet
> I know how to play.
> When the night gets dark as jet
> Every cat looks gray.

(*He sings the last verse again, dancing to the rhythm.* FIGARO *comes in behind him and mimics his movements from behind. Noticing* FIGARO:) Hello, Mr. Barber. Step forward. You are a charming fellow.

FIGARO (*bowing*): Sir, it's true that my mother said so once, but since then I've become somewhat less sightly. (*Aside, to the* COUNT.) Everything is under control, my lord.

(*During this scene, the* COUNT *tries his hardest to talk to* ROSINE, *but after* FIGARO's *entrance*, BARTHOLO *becomes watchful, and the* COUNT *and* ROSINE *have to play a sort of dumb game during the following exchange of dialogue.*)

BARTHOLO: Have you come back to purge and bleed and drug my household again?

FIGARO: Unfortunately, sir, not every day is a holiday, but when it comes to doing those routine little things that have to be done, I'm always at your command. . . .

BARTHOLO: Oh, yes? Then what do you say, Mr. Activity, to that poor creature who is yawning and falling asleep on his feet? Or to the other poor fellow who has been sneezing his nose off for the last three hours?

FIGARO: What would I say to them? Well, to the one who is sneezing, I would say: "God bless you." And to the one who is falling asleep, I would say: "Go to bed." And I wouldn't charge either of them for the advice.

BARTHOLO: No, but you'll charge them for the bleeding and the drugs, won't you? And what about my poor, blind mule, with his eyes blocked up by a poultice?

FIGARO: That won't stop him from seeing anything that he missed before.

BARTHOLO: Just let me find it on the bill, that's all. I don't believe in these expensive jokes.

FIGARO: Men have hardly any choice between stupidity and folly; so where I can't make a profit, I try to make some pleasure. Long live joy. Who knows if the world will last for another three weeks?

BARTHOLO: It would be better for both of us, Mr. Reason-Twister, if you paid me my hundred crowns without any more evasion.

FIGARO: Do you doubt my honesty, sir? I would never deny that I owe you one hundred crowns. I would rather owe you them for the rest of my life.

BARTHOLO: And by the way, how did your daughter like the candies?

FIGARO: What candies are you talking about?

BARTHOLO: The ones you took in the paper cone this morning.

FIGARO: Damned if I remember . . .

ROSINE (*interrupting*): I hope you remembered to give them to her, Mr. Figaro. I asked you to tell her they were from me.

FIGARO: Oh, the candies. The candies from this morning. Of course. I'm so stupid. I'd forgotten all about them. They were excellent, madam, delicious.

BARTHOLO: Yes, excellent, delicious! As delicious as the taste of your own words, when you have to eat them. Words seem to be your stock-in-trade.

FIGARO: What's wrong now, sir?

BARTHOLO: A fine reputation you're giving yourself.

FIGARO: A high reputation, I hope, sir.

BARTHOLO: Make sure you're not underneath when it starts to fall, sir.

FIGARO: I'll take your advice, sir.

BARTHOLO: Don't turn away from me, sir. When I argue with a fool, I never give in.

FIGARO: We differ there, sir. I always give in. (*Turns his back on* BARTHOLO.)

BARTHOLO: What was that he said, Señor Alonzo?

FIGARO: You think you're talking to some village barber, who can handle nothing but a razor. But I, sir, wield a pen too. When I was in Madrid, if it hadn't been for those envious . . .

BARTHOLO: You should have stayed in Madrid. Why did you change your profession?

FIGARO: I had no choice. Put yourself in my place.

BARTHOLO: Not likely. I'd be saying such idiotic things.

FIGARO: You haven't started too badly. I appeal to your colleague who is daydreaming over there to bear me out.

COUNT: I am not his colleague.

FIGARO: Oh? I saw you here and assumed that you were working together.

BARTHOLO (*angrily*): What have you come for? Have you brought the young lady another letter? Perhaps I should step outside.

FIGARO: You are so rude to the lower classes. No, sir, I came in order to shave you, that's all. Isn't today your day?

BARTHOLO: Come back some other time.

FIGARO: What other time? Tomorrow morning, I have to give all the men in the barracks their laxatives. I have an exclusive contract; I had to bribe heavily to get it. So I have no time to waste. Would you like to go into your room?

BARTHOLO: No, I would not. Why can't you shave me in here?

ROSINE (*scornfully*):   How gentlemanly! Why not in my room?

BARTHOLO: Don't be annoyed, my dear. You still have to finish your lesson. I didn't want to miss the pleasure of hearing you.

FIGARO (*aside, to the* COUNT):   We'll never get him out of here. (*Aloud.*) Lively! Puberty! Come on! Water, a basin and everything else I need to shave the doctor.

BARTHOLO: It won't do you any good to call them. I had to send them to bed, exhausted, harassed, and helpless after your treatment.

FIGARO: All right, I'll get the things myself. They are in your room, aren't they? (*Aside to the* COUNT.) I'll soon get him outside.

BARTHOLO (*takes out his bunch of keys, then reflects*):   No, I'll go. (*Aside to the* COUNT, *as he goes out.*) Keep an eye on them. (*Exit.*)

FIGARO: We missed a great opportunity there. He was going to give me his key ring. I think the window key is on it.

ROSINE: Yes, it's the brand-new one.

(BARTHOLO *comes back.*)

BARTHOLO (*aside*):   I don't know what I was thinking of, to let that crafty barber stay in here. (*Aloud.*) Here. (*Gives him the bunch of keys.*) In my room, under the desk. Don't touch anything else.

FIGARO: It would serve you right if I did, you're so suspicious. (*Aside, as he goes out fingering the key.*) See how Heaven helps the righteous. (*Exit.*)

BARTHOLO (*aside, to the* COUNT):   He's the wretch who took the letter to the count.

COUNT: He looks irresponsible to me.

BARTHOLO: He won't catch me again.

COUNT: I'm sure the worst is over.

BARTHOLO: Everything considered, I thought it was safer to send him to my room than to leave him here with her.

COUNT: They couldn't have said anything. I would have overheard.

ROSINE: Gentlemen, it isn't very polite to keep whispering. What about my lesson?

(*A noise, off, as of breaking china.*)

BARTHOLO: What was that crash? That clumsy barber must have dropped everything on the stairs. . . . My finest china! (*He runs out.*)

COUNT: Figaro has found a way to give us a moment together. I think I know how to rescue you, if you will listen to these instructions.

ROSINE: Of course, Lindor.

COUNT: I'll climb up to your window. I received your letter this morning, but I was forced to say that . . .

(BARTHOLO *and* FIGARO *come back.*)

BARTHOLO: I was right. Everything is broken, shattered.

FIGARO: It was hard luck. I couldn't see a thing on the stairs. (*He shows the key to the* COUNT.) As I was coming up, the key got caught in the banister rail . . .

BARTHOLO: Why didn't you take more care? The key got caught! Clever man!

FIGARO: Find somebody cleverer, then.

(DON BAZILE *comes in.*)

ROSINE: Don Bazile!

COUNT (*aside*): That's a nuisance.

FIGARO (*aside*): That's a disaster.

BARTHOLO: Ah, Bazile, my friend, I'm glad you're fit again. No after-effects from your illness, eh? I was very worried by what Señor Alonzo told me. Ask him if I wasn't ready to rush off to see you. If he hadn't kept me from going . . .

BAZILE: Señor Alonzo?

FIGARO (*stamping on the floor*): Why do I have to put up with all these hindrances? Two hours for one rotten beard. What kind of a customer are you?

BAZILE (*looking around in bewilderment*): Gentlemen, will you please explain to me—

FIGARO: No. You can talk to him after I go.

BAZILE: But I must . . .

COUNT: You must not say one word, Bazile. Do you think you're telling the doctor anything he doesn't already know? I told him that you asked me to give the music lesson for you.

BAZILE: The music lesson? Alonzo? What is this . . . ?

ROSINE: Hush. Quiet.

BAZILE: Are you in this too?

COUNT (*aside, to* BARTHOLO): Tell him about our arrangement.

BARTHOLO (*aside, to* DON BAZILE): Don't give us away, Bazile, by saying that he isn't your pupil. You'll spoil everything.

BAZILE: My pupil . . . ? (*Quietly.*) I came to tell you that the count has moved to . . .

BARTHOLO: Yes, I know. Keep quiet.

BAZILE: Who told you?

BARTHOLO: He did, of course.

COUNT (*joining in quietly*): Of course I did. Just listen.

ROSINE (*quietly to* BAZILE): Is it so hard for you to keep quiet?

FIGARO (*quietly to* BAZILE): Great oaf. He's deaf.

BAZILE: Who the devil's deceiving whom? Everybody's in on the secret.

BARTHOLO (*aloud*): What happened with the lawyer?

FIGARO: He has the whole evening to tell you about the lawyer.

BARTHOLO: Just one thing: are you satisfied with him?

BAZILE (*bewildered*): With the lawyer?

COUNT (*smiling*): Haven't you seen him?

BAZILE (*irritated now*): No, I haven't seen him.

COUNT (*quietly to* BARTHOLO): Do you want him to explain everything in front of her? Send him away.

BARTHOLO (*quietly, to the* COUNT): You're right. (*To* BAZILE.) But what was that illness that took you suddenly?

BAZILE (*furiously*): I don't know what you're talking about.

COUNT (*slipping him a purse*): The doctor means, why did you come here when you weren't well?

FIGARO: He's as white as a corpse.

BAZILE (*looking at the purse*): I'm beginning to understand.

COUNT: Put yourself to bed, my dear Bazile. You don't look fit and we're worried about you. Go to bed.

FIGARO: His face is all drawn. Go to bed.

BARTHOLO: On my word, you could see the fever from a mile away. Go to bed.

ROSINE: Why did you come out? It may be catching. Go to bed.

BAZILE: I think I'd better go to bed.

EVERYBODY: Yes. Go to bed.

BAZILE (*staring at them in turn*): As a matter of fact, I do think it might be wise for me to go home. I don't feel quite up to my ordinary standards.

BARTHOLO: Till tomorrow, then—if you are better.

COUNT: Bazile, I shall be round to see you early.

FIGARO: Take it from me: Your bed should be good and warm.

ROSINE: Good night, Don Bazile.

BAZILE (*aside*):   God help me, I don't understand a thing. If it weren't for this purse . . .

EVERYBODY: Good night, Bazile, good night.

BAZILE: If you all say so. Good night. (*They all see him to the door.*)

BARTHOLO (*professionally*):   That man is definitely not well.

ROSINE: His eyes were rolling.

COUNT: It's a chill of some kind.

FIGARO: Did you see how he was muttering to himself? As if we weren't here? (*to* BARTHOLO.) Well, are you ready now? (*Sits him in a chair and puts a sheet around him; they are at the other end of the room from the* COUNT *and* ROSINE.)

COUNT: Before we conclude the lesson, madam, I must mention one thing that will be essential to the progress of your technique in this art that I am trying to teach you. (*He whispers to her.*)

BARTHOLO (*to* FIGARO):   You seem to be standing in my way deliberately, to stop me from seeing . . .

COUNT (*to* ROSINE):   We have the key to the window. We'll be here at midnight.

FIGARO (*tucking the sheet around* BARTHOLO's *neck*): From seeing what? If it were a dancing lesson, I'd let you see. But a singing lesson? Oh, oh!

BARTHOLO: What's wrong?

FIGARO: Something went in my eye. (*Puts his head near.*)

BARTHOLO: Don't rub it.

FIGARO: The left eye. Do you think you could get it out?

(BARTHOLO *takes* FIGARO's *head, looks over it and sees the* COUNT *and* ROSINE *whispering. He pushes* FIGARO *violently away and goes behind the others to listen to their conversation.*)

COUNT: About your letter: I needed an excuse to stay here . . .

FIGARO: Ahem, ahem.

COUNT: My disguise didn't seem to be working again . . .

BARTHOLO (*coming between them*):   So your disguise didn't seem to be working . . .

ROSINE: Oh!

BARTHOLO: Very good. In front of me, under my very eyes, you dare to commit such an outrage!

COUNT: What is the matter, sir?

BARTHOLO: Alonzo, eh? It looks like treachery to me.

COUNT: Senor Bartholo, if you often behave in this ridiculous way, I am not surprised that the young lady is reluctant to be your wife.

ROSINE: His wife? What? To spend my days with a jealous old man who offers me slavery for happiness?

BARTHOLO: How dare you say that!

ROSINE: Say it? I'll shout it! I will give my heart and my hand to anybody who can rescue me from this loathsome prison. (*She goes out.*)

BARTHOLO: I'm choking with anger.

COUNT: It is difficult, sir, for a young woman—

FIGARO: Yes, a young woman and an old man, that's what's troubling his senile head.

BARTHOLO: I caught them in the act. You damn barber, I'd like to . . .

FIGARO: I'm getting out. He's mad.

COUNT: So am I. He is mad. (*They go out.*)

BARTHOLO: Mad, am I? Crooks, rogues, slaves of Satan, trying to turn my house into hell. I hope he carries you all off. Mad, am I? I saw them as clearly as I can see this desk . . . and then they face me brazenly. The only man who can tell me what has really happened is Bazile. Come here, somebody. . . . Oh, I forgot; there's nobody. A neighbor, a passer-by, it doesn't matter. It's enough to make me mind my lose—lose my mind!

ACT IV

(During the entr'acte music, the sounds of a storm are heard. When the curtain rises the stage is dark. BARTHOLO enters, followed by DON BAZILE, with a lantern in his hand.)

BARTHOLO: What's this, Bazile? You don't know him? How is that possible?

BAZILE: If you asked me a hundred times, I'd give you the same answer. If he handed you Rosine's letter, he must be one of the count's messengers. But to judge by the magnificent sum of money he gave me, he could even be the count himself.

BARTHOLO: How can we know? By the way, that money he gave you—why did you take it?

BAZILE: He seemed to be in league with you. I didn't know what was going on. And whenever it's difficult for me to make up my mind about anything, a purse always convinces me. Besides, as the proverb goes: whatever is worth taking . . .

BARTHOLO: I know: is worth . . .

BAZILE: Keeping.

BARTHOLO *(surprised)*: You mean: is worth earning.

BAZILE: I arrange my proverbs to suit circumstances. Variations on a theme. But to get back to the point: how far are you prepared to go?

BARTHOLO: In my place, Bazile, wouldn't you go all out to get her?

BAZILE: No, I would not, Doctor. When it comes to property, ownership is not important; it's enjoyment that makes a man happy. I suggest that if you marry a woman who doesn't love you, you leave yourself open—

BARTHOLO: To deception?

BAZILE *(laughing)*: Well, sir, there have been a good number of deceptions this year. I wouldn't put myself out to win a heart that doesn't want me.

BARTHOLO: You are you. It is better for her to weep with me than for me to die without her.

BAZILE: If it's life or death to you, Doctor, then marry her.

BARTHOLO: I intend to. Tonight.

BAZILE: Good-by, then. But remember, when you are talking to her about Figaro and the count, make them seem blacker than hell.

BARTHOLO: Leave it to me.

BAZILE: It's slander, Doctor. Slander. You can't beat it.

BARTHOLO: Here is Rosine's letter; that fellow Alonzo gave it to me. He showed me it without realizing that I could make good use of it.

BAZILE: Good-by; we'll all be here at four o'clock.

BARTHOLO: Why not earlier?

BAZILE: Impossible; the notary is booked.

BARTHOLO: For a marriage?

BAZILE: Yes, at the barber Figaro's house. His niece is getting married.

BARTHOLO: He hasn't got a niece.

BAZILE: He told the notary that he has.

BARTHOLO: I'll swear he's involved in this plot. What is he up to now?

BAZILE: Do you think that . . . ?

BARTHOLO: Those people are clever. I'm not comfortable about this. Go back to the notary and bring him here with you at once.

BAZILE: It's raining; the weather is fierce; but nothing can hold Don Bazile back when he is under contract. Where are you going?

BARTHOLO: To see you out. Figaro has disabled all my servants. I am alone here.

BAZILE: I have my lantern.

BARTHOLO: Here is my master key. I'll wait for you. Whatever happens, nobody but the notary and yourself will be able to come in.

BAZILE: With those precautions, you can't go wrong.

(*They go out. Enter* ROSINE.)

ROSINE: I thought I heard somebody talking. Midnight has struck and Lindor has not come. This bad weather should have helped him. . . . He was sure of not meeting anybody. Ah, Lindor, if you have let me down . . . What is that noise? Oh, it's my guardian. I'll go back inside.

BARTHOLO (*holding up a lamp*): Rosine, since you aren't in your room . . .

ROSINE: I am just going to bed.

BARTHOLO: You won't sleep in this weather, and I have some urgent matters to discuss.

ROSINE: What do you want with me, sir? Isn't it enough to be tormented by you in daylight?

BARTHOLO: Listen to me, Rosine.

ROSINE: I will—tomorrow.

BARTHOLO: One moment, that's all. Please.

ROSINE (*aside*): If he has found out . . .

BARTHOLO (*showing her the letter*): Do you recognize this letter?

ROSINE (*startled*): Where did you get it?

BARTHOLO: I am not going to reproach you, Rosine; at your age a person makes mistakes. But I am your friend, believe me.

ROSINE: I don't want to talk to you any more.

BARTHOLO: This letter, which you wrote to Count Almaviva . . .

ROSINE: To Count Almaviva?

BARTHOLO: You can see what kind of a man he is. As soon as he received it, he gave it to another woman as a keepsake.

ROSINE: Count Almaviva!

BARTHOLO: You can hardly believe this, can you? You are young and inexperienced and gullible. But you were being drawn into a trap. This woman has told me everything; apparently she regards you as a rival. It makes me shudder. This was a plot by Almaviva, Figaro, and this Alonzo, who claimed to be a pupil of Bazile; that is not his real name; he is only an agent for the count. They were planning to mislead you and ruin your name.

ROSINE: Horrible. What, Lindor, that pleasant young man . . . ?

BARTHOLO: Ah, (*aside*) his name is Lindor. . . .

ROSINE: And doing it for Count Almaviva . . . for another man . . .

BARTHOLO: That's what I was told when I was given this letter.

ROSINE: What an indignity! A man has deceived me. He will be punished for it. Sir, you wanted to marry me?

BARTHOLO: You know how deep my feelings are.

ROSINE: If they have not changed, I am yours.

BARTHOLO: Wonderful. The notary will be here tonight.

ROSINE: There is something else. Oh, God, I have been

so humiliated! He is going to come in through that window. He and Figaro stole the key from you.

BARTHOLO (*looking at the key ring*): So they did, the scoundrels. Don't worry, my child, I won't leave you.

ROSINE: What if they are armed?

BARTHOLO: You may be right. I would lose my revenge. Go up to Marceline's room and double-lock yourself in. I'll go out and get help, and wait for them outside the house. I'll have them arrested as thieves. We'll be revenged and rescued at the same time: a double pleasure. Trust my affection; I shall make you happy again.

ROSINE: Please forgive my mistakes. I have been punished enough.

BARTHOLO: Now to lay the ambush. I know how to deal with them. (*Exit.*)

ROSINE: He thinks he can make me happy again when I am so unhappy. (*She cries into her handkerchief.*) What can I do? Lindor will be here any moment. I'd like to stay and argue with him, to see how he tries to trick me. That is what I need to save myself from him. I must. A noble face, a gentle manner, a tender voice . . . and he is nothing but a mercenary. I am so unhappy. . . . What's that? Somebody is opening the window. (*She runs out.*)

(*The* COUNT *appears at the window, with* FIGARO; *they are wearing cloaks.*)

FIGARO (*outside*): Somebody ran away. Shall I go in?

COUNT (*outside*): A man?

FIGARO: No.

COUNT: It was Rosine. Your face frightened her away.

FIGARO: I believe it. (*Jumps into the room.*) Well, here we are, in spite of the rain, thunder, and lightning.

COUNT: Help me in. (*He jumps inside.*) Victory at last.

FIGARO (*throwing off his cloak*): We're soaked through. Charming weather for fortune hunting. What do you think of this night, my lord?

COUNT: For a lover, superb.

FIGARO: Yes, but for an accomplice . . . ? And suppose we're caught here?

COUNT: You're with me, aren't you? I'm worried about something else: how to persuade her to leave this house with us immediately.

FIGARO: As far as the fair sex is concerned, you have the three big passions on your side: love, hatred, and fear.

COUNT (*looking into the darkness*): How can I tell her

right out that the notary is waiting at your house to marry us? She'll think I'm too bold; she'll say it's a risk.

FIGARO: If she says you're too bold, you can say she's cruel. Women love to be called cruel. And if she loves you as much as you hope, tell her who you are. Then she won't doubt your feelings.

(FIGARO *lights the candles on the table.*)

COUNT: Here she is. My lovely Rosine.

ROSINE (*in a cool voice*): I was beginning to fear that you were not coming, sir.

COUNT: A charming fear. I don't wish to take advantage of the circumstances; I am offering you a share in my poverty; but wherever you choose to live, I swear on my honor . . .

ROSINE: Sir, you would not be here if you were not taking my heart with my hand. It is not your fault if the circumstances are . . . irregular.

COUNT: Rosine, can you accept the companionship of a man without fortune or birth?

ROSINE: Fortune, birth! These are things that come by chance. Simply assure me that your intentions are pure. . . .

COUNT (*kneeling*): Rosine, I adore you.

ROSINE: Stop! You dare to say that, to lie? You adore me! I'm not in danger any longer. I was waiting for that word. I detest you. But before I leave you to your remorse (*crying*) I want you to know that I did love you; I thought I would be happy sharing your poverty. I was ready to leave everything and follow you. But you took advantage of my trust. I know now that you were working for this despicable Count Almaviva, that you were going to sell me to him. Do you recognize this letter?

COUNT: Did your guardian give it back to you?

ROSINE: Yes, and I am grateful to him.

COUNT: I am so glad of the chance to explain it to you. I gave it to him to win his confidence, and I have been trying to tell you about it. It is true then, Rosine, that you love me?

FIGARO: My lord, you wanted a woman who would love you for yourself. . . .

ROSINE: What did he say? "My lord"?

COUNT (*throwing off his cloak, and appearing in magnificent costume*): My darling, now I can tell you the truth; I am not Lindor; I am Count Almaviva. I am dying of love; I have spent six months trying to find you.

ROSINE (*slumping into his arms*):   Ah!

COUNT: Figaro!

FIGARO: Nothing to get upset about, my lord. She's overcome with joy, and that's the best way to be overcome. There you are, she's coming to already. God, she's beautiful.

ROSINE: Ah, Lindor—I mean, my lord—I have been wicked. I promised to marry my guardian tonight.

COUNT: Rosine . . .

ROSINE: I was nearly punished: I would have spent my life hating you. The worst fate of all, Lindor, is to hate when one was made to love.

FIGARO (*at the window*):   My lord, they've cut off our escape. The ladder is gone.

COUNT: Gone?

ROSINE: It's the doctor. I believed him. I told him everything; I gave away the whole story. He knows that you are here, and he is coming up with the police.

FIGARO: They're opening the street door.

ROSINE: Lindor . . . (*She runs into his arms.*)

COUNT: Rosine, you love me, and I am not afraid of anybody. You will be my wife. And that will be our first punishment on the old man. . . .

ROSINE: No, Lindor. Have pity on him. My heart is too full of love to leave any room for vengeance.

(*Enter* DON BAZILE *and* NOTARY.)

FIGARO: It's our notary, my lord.

COUNT: And Bartholo's friend Bazile with him.

BAZILE: What's happening?

FIGARO: This is lucky. How did you . . . ?

BAZILE: This is a mistake. How did you . . . ?

NOTARY: Are these the happy people who are to be conjoined?

COUNT: Yes, sir. You were supposed to marry this young lady and me tonight at Figaro's house; but we have chosen this house instead, for reasons that we will explain. Have you got the contract?

NOTARY: Have I the honor of addressing His Excellency Count Almaviva?

FIGARO: You have.

BAZILE (*aside*):   If that's why he gave me the master key . . .

NOTARY: I have two marriage contracts, my lord. We must not confuse them. This one is yours; and here is Señor Bartholo's. He is also going to marry a young lady named Rosine. Apparently, the two ladies are sisters who have the same name.

COUNT: Let's sign the contract, anyway. Perhaps Don Bazile will sign as the second witness? (*The* COUNT *and* ROSINE *sign.*)

BAZILE: But Your Excellency, I don't understand. . . .

COUNT: My dear Bazile, you are upset by a nothing, and astonished by everything.

BAZILE: But my lord, if the doctor . . .

COUNT (*throwing him a purse*): Don't be awkward. Sign quickly.

BAZILE: Ah, but . . .

FIGARO: What's the difficulty now?

BAZILE (*hefting the purse*): There isn't any. But when I give my word, I have to have a heavy reason for breaking it. (*He signs.*)

(*Enter* BARTHOLO, *with an* ALCALDE [*Spanish magistrate*], POLICEMEN, *and* SERVANTS *with torches.*)

BARTHOLO (*seeing the* COUNT *kissing* ROSINE'*s hand and* FIGARO *embracing* DON BAZILE): Rosine, with these scoundrels! (*Grabs the* NOTARY *by the throat.*) Arrest the lot of them. I've got this one.

NOTARY: I am your notary.

BAZILE: He's your notary. Are you joking?

BARTHOLO: How did you come to be in here?

BAZILE: How did you come to be out of here?

ALCALDE (*pointing to* FIGARO): One moment. I know this man. What are you doing in this house at this late hour?

FIGARO: This early hour, you mean. It's nearer morning than night. I came with His Excellency my lord the Count Almaviva.

BARTHOLO: Almaviva!

ALCALDE: Then these people are not thieves?

BARTHOLO: Forget about that now. (*To the* COUNT.) Anywhere else, my lord, I am your humble servant, but in my house, rank does not mean anything, and I ask you to leave.

COUNT: No, rank doesn't mean anything here; I have nothing over you except Rosine's preference. She has just given me her hand.

BARTHOLO: Is that true, Rosine?

ROSINE: Quite true. Why are you surprised? Didn't I say that I would punish the man who deceived me?

BAZILE: You see, Doctor. I told you it was the count himself.

BARTHOLO: I don't care about that. This marriage is ridiculous. Where are the witnesses?

NOTARY: Everything was in order. I called on these two gentlemen to assist me.

BARTHOLO: What! Bazile, you signed?

BAZILE: What else could I do? This man (*indicating the* COUNT) always has his pockets full of irresistible arguments.

BARTHOLO: I don't give a damn for his arguments. I will use my authority.

COUNT: You have lost it by abusing it.

BARTHOLO: The young lady is a minor.

FIGARO: She has just come of age.

BARTHOLO: Who is talking to you, crook?

COUNT: The young lady is noble and beautiful. I am a man of rank, and I am young and rich. She is now my wife. Is anybody prepared to dispute this marriage which honors us both?

BARTHOLO: I will not give her up.

COUNT: She does not belong to you any more. I shall ask the law, which you were kind enough to bring, to decide whether or not she should be protected against your violence. Our magistrates are the true guardians of the oppressed.

ALCALDE: That is correct. This man's resistance to an honorable marriage indicates that there may have been some misappropriation of his ward's property. He will have to give a full account of her possessions.

COUNT: As long as he agrees to the marriage, I won't pursue this any further. He can keep all property.

FIGARO: Except my bill for one hundred crowns. Let's not lose our heads about this.

BARTHOLO: They were all against me. I stuck my head into a wasp's nest.

BAZILE: You've got it out of a wasp's nest. The girl is gone—but the money remains. The money, old man.

BARTHOLO: Leave me alone, Bazile. All you think of is money. What do I care about money? Do you think money is my only motive? (*He signs.*)

FIGARO: You see, my lord, these two belong to the same family.

NOTARY: But, gentlemen, I am a little bewildered. Are there not two young ladies with the same name?

FIGARO: No, sir. They are only one.

BARTHOLO: And after I took away the ladder to make sure of my marriage! I lost because I was not cautious enough.

FIGARO: Not clever enough. Let's admit it, Doctor: when love and youth unite to deceive an old man, anything he does to try to stop them can only be called a useless precaution. . . .

EUGENE LABICHE (1815–1888)
AND A. DELACOUR

Labiche, born and raised in Paris, came from what a social
psychologist might call the lower-middle-to-lower-middle-
middle class. Not much is known—or if known, recorded
—of his personal life. He was evidently the kind of
child every parent secretly wishes for. He had a placid
temper and a gay but obedient disposition. He was in the
habit of making quietly self-deprecating remarks about himself and humorous comments about others without, on the
one hand, talking about himself unduly or, on the other
hand, giving offense. He was not studious and never particularly devoted to Latin or Greek or "cultural" matters in
general, but he had a sharp enough mind and retentive
enough memory to pass examinations and to bring home
good reports from his school, the Collège Bourbon. When
his father suggested that he should study law, Eugène
went unprotestingly to the law courses and came through
with above-average grades. When his father thought that
Eugène should take the standard, mind-broadening tour
through Switzerland, Italy, and Sicily before settling down
to a career, Eugène obediently left home, took the pre-
scribed route and returned with a presumably broader mind.
    At twenty, he had several friends who were journalists
and were able to help him to find work with a number of
small papers, including *Chérubin* and *La Gazette des
Théâtres.* His parents did not mind that he had not gone
into a legal practice. After all, he was not a bohemian: he
dressed, talked, thought, and behaved like a satisfactory
bourgeois; he did not associate with any red-vested roman-
tics; he brought home a respectable wage; he had no grudges
against anybody, no enemies; he ate whatever his mother
cooked and relished it.
    When he was twenty-four, Labiche published a humorous
novel, *La Clef des Champs* (*The Key of the Fields*): nobody
was surprised, nobody was annoyed. Two years later, he
wrote his first play, *Monsieur de Coyllon,* or *The Infinitely*

Polite Man, in collaboration with two established playwrights whom he had met on the outskirts of Parisian theater life. The play did not generate any ripples of talk or influence, but it did give a break to Grassot, a comedian who later became very famous. Labiche was not discouraged. He enjoyed his "scribbling," as he called it, and went on to scribble some more little plays which were concerned with lower-middle-middle-class merchants, their foibles and their problems in getting their daughters married and dowered. The plays were designed for laughs and were written on a personal or local level, ignoring the cultural, political, and economic revolutions going on around them at the instigation of such men as Hugo, Balzac, Delacroix, Courbet, Baudelaire, Louis Blanc, and Saint-Simon. They were rather like today's domestic comedies on television, storms in suburban teacups, sometimes flat enough to be in saucers.

Labiche hit his stride in 1848 (the year in which the French monarchy collapsed—February—and recovered—December) with a one-act called *Young Man in a Hurry,* but another play performed the same year, *The Champenois Club,* was more satirical and biting—Labiche was discernibly laughing *at* the middle classes, and not with them—and it flopped. Labiche was by now popular with theater managers, however. He could turn out a slick little laughing-piece at a few days' notice, and was always willing to rewrite to order.

In 1851 he wrote his first full-length play, a five-act, in collaboration with one of his early partners. *The Italian Straw Hat* was an immediate hit. Francisque Sarcey, the most influential reviewer of the mid-nineteenth century, called it a "revolution in vaudeville," and it has gone on to become the most popular comedy of this type in French literature, as well as a remarkable silent motion picture (1927) under the direction of René Clair. The original production of *Le Chapeau de Paille d'Italie* enjoyed three hundred performances. The following year Labiche wrote and had staged six plays and sketches (*pochades*), all to order; he followed them with *The Vultures in Pursuit,* another five-act, written with Marc-Michel, in which the satirical spirit returned and the men of the money market were seen as flesh-eating ravens or vultures. But the message was a little too personal for most of the audience and the play failed badly.

Nevertheless, Labiche was now pulling in a good income from his writing, enough, at any rate, to buy him a substantial acreage of farming-and-hunting property in La Sologne, about eighty miles south of Paris and twenty-five miles east-southeast of Orléans in the great bend of the Loire River. By this time (1853), he was married and had a family as well as a desire to promote himself to the rank of gentleman-farmer.

Having conquered the "vaudeville" formula, Labiche again tried to break away from it, but met with only lukewarm receptions for *Les Marquises de la Fourchette* and *The Miser in Yellow Gloves*. But his next play, a four-act, *Monsieur Perrichon's Journey* (1860), was so enthusiastically received by public and reviewers alike that Labiche had indisputably become the first comic dramatist of his day. In the next four years he wrote twenty-odd plays, culminating in *Myself,* which was commissioned by the Comédie-Française, and earlier that same year (1864) *Pots of Money (La Cagnotte,* which means literally, "the kitty"), the last of his three five-act plays, and subsequently one of the most popular of Labiche's works in France.

From 1865 on, Labiche spent most of his time on his estate in La Sologne, coming back to Paris only for the rehearsals of his plays. He was elected mayor of the commune and seemed to enjoy his local duties. In 1870, when the Prussians invaded France, Labiche managed to secure from them a promise not to shoot hostages by claiming that he would rather face shooting himself than deliver up guerrillas. The Prussians did not press him.

In 1875 Philippe Gille, a journalist, collaborated with him on *Gladiator's Thirty Millions,* which did not do very well, although a young actress named Sarah Bernhardt was warmly applauded in the role of Suzanne, the *cocotte.* The following year he collaborated with Émile Augier, his friend, counselor and co-playwright, on *The Martin Prize,* a three-act comedy, and with Legouvé on a one-act, *Grasshopper Among the Ants.* And this was his last play. At the age of sixty-one Labiche resolutely gave up writing, saying that it was "better to retire from the theater too soon than too late." He passed the remaining thirteen years of his life on his farms where, according to Augier, he grew wheat and pine-trees, cattle and sheep, ate and drank as heavily and zestfully as ever—he was a big, stout man—and took part in local activities with great fervor.

Augier persuaded him to reprint his complete works in one series; his plays had been published by twenty-six different houses. Labiche agreed reluctantly, and only on condition that Augier would write the preface, which he did, claiming that the plays gain 100 per cent in reading over performance, since they are then divorced from stage trickery and business. This is rather like saying that a conjuror can perform better without an audience because then nobody can see what he is up to.

Actually, only 57 of Labiche's total of 160 or so plays were included in the *Complete Works;* they had been written with twenty different collaborators, with all of whom Labiche was still on good terms. (Of the plays included in the *Complete Works,* only six were written by Labiche alone, and they are all one-acts.)

After the publication of the *Complete Works,* there was a revival of interest in Labiche's plays, particularly the earlier successes like *The Italian Straw Hat, Monsieur Perrichon's Journey,* and *Pots of Money.* As a result, Labiche was proposed for the French Academy and took his seat in November 1880. It is not known if he made any contributions to the Academy; he remained a modest, pleasantly mannered man, who never traded on his reputation. In 1888 he died at home on his estate, and was nationally mourned.

A LIST OF LABICHE'S PRINCIPAL PLAYS:

(Those included here represent a tiny fraction of Labiche's output. He did not himself consider most of the others worth reprinting in his *Complete Works.*)

The Italian Straw Hat (1851), *The Vultures in Pursuit* (1853), *The Affair in the Rue de Lourcine* (1857), *The Miser in Yellow Gloves* (1858), *A Gentleman Has Burned a Lady* (1858), *M. Perrichon's Journey* (also translated under a multitude of other titles, 1860), *Dust in Your Eyes* (1861), *M. Montaudouin's 37 Sous* (1862), *Célimare the Beloved* (1863), *Myself* (1864), *Pots of Money* (1864), *Grammar* (1867), *The Happiest of the Three* (1870), *Must It Be Said?* (1872), *Twenty-Nine Degrees in the Shade* (1873), *Gladiator's Thirty Millions* (1875), *The Martin Prize* (1876), *Grasshopper Among the Ants* (1876).

SUGGESTIONS FOR FURTHER READING
ON LABICHE:

Very little has been written about Labiche in English. Émile Augier's preface to Labiche's *Complete Works,* translated by Mary Douglas Dirks, appears in *The Tulane Drama Review*, Winter 1959. The only biography is in French, *Eugène Labiche, Sa Vie, Son Oeuvre*, by Philippe Soupault (Editions du Sagittaire, 1945). Reviews of many Labiche plays can be found in Francisque Sarcey: *Forty Years of Theatre*.

POTS OF MONEY
(LA CAGNOTTE)

A Comedy in Five Acts

by Eugène Labiche and A. Delacour

FIRST PERFORMED IN PARIS IN 1864

CHARACTERS [1]

BOURSEY, *a man of independent means*
DANNE, *a rich farmer*
CORDEN, *a pharmacist*
SYLVAIN, *son of Danne*
FELIX, *a young lawyer*
PENURI, *a tax collector*
POCHE, *a marriage broker*
CHUTE, *an assistant police commissioner*
LEONIDA, *sister of Boursey*
BLANCHE, *daughter of Boursey*
BENJAMIN, *a waiter*
JOSEPH, *servant of Poche*
TRICOT, *a fruit merchant*
MADAME CARAMEL, *a grocer*
SECOND WAITER
THIRD WAITER
POLICEMAN

France in the 1860's. The first act takes place in the village of Endives-Under-Glass; the other four acts, in Paris.

[1] Some of the characters' names have been slightly modified from the French.

ACT I

(*A provincial living room in the village of Endives-Under-Glass.* BLANCHE *and* LEONIDA *are seated round a small table, knitting or crocheting.* PENURI *is reading a newspaper.* BOURSEY, DANNE, CORDEN, *and* FELIX *are playing cards.*)

BLANCHE: Aren't you joining the card game this evening, Aunt Leonida?

LEONIDA: Yes, very shortly.

FELIX: It's my turn to drop out. You can take my place in five minutes.

LEONIDA: It's not your turn. It's somebody else's. But he doesn't seem to be moving.

CORDEN: Don't think I didn't hear that.

PENURI: Well, well! (*Lowering the newspaper.*) Here's a curious advertisement.

EVERYBODY: What's that?

PENURI: Listen. "Young, attractive, majestic lady, with annual income of five thousand francs, bracket, from well-selected shares, close the bracket, would like to meet honest man, widower or bachelor, with romantic disposition. Must be in good health, reasonably provided, and not too old. No fortune necessary. Objective: marriage and a modest home in a small, well-situated town. For information, write to Box 44, care of this newspaper, and enclose stamped, addressed envelope. No frivolous replies, please."

BOURSEY: That's an old one. It's been appearing in the paper, on and off, for three years now. I pass. My tooth is killing me.

PENURI: Imagine anybody replying to that kind of an advertisement. It's indecent. The woman is shameless.

LEONIDA: I don't see anything wrong with it. A poor, forgotten person, sitting out her life in some corner of the provinces, waiting for happiness. And somewhere else a man, alone, who could be that happiness. And suddenly, perhaps, the personal column brings them together.

79

CORDEN: They say there have been some nice matches through the personal column. As a bachelor, I must say I read it from time to time and dream all sorts of dreams. . . .

DANNE: Bunkum! If you want to marry somebody you hang about together and it happens naturally. Take me: when I came across my late wife and took a fancy to her we started going together right away. I went to her house, she came to my house, and before we knew it—bang! That's how people get married.

BOURSEY: Come on, come on. Let's get back to the game.

LEONIDA (standing up): Nine-fifteen. My turn.

CORDEN: Wait till we finish one more hand.

FELIX: No, I'll drop out. You can take over my hand. (He changes seats with LEONIDA.)

CORDEN: You want to keep playing all the time. I never met such a greedy cardplayer.

LEONIDA: What are you complaining about? You're still in the game, aren't you? Show some manners for a change. If you can.

CORDEN: Listen to who's talking. The most bloodthirsty cardplayer in—

BOURSEY: Stop it! You're always squabbling, you two. Remember you're the godmother and godfather of the bell-ringer's son. Try to behave like a godmother and godfather.

DANNE (to LEONIDA): He did give you that diamond pendant, after the christening.

CORDEN: Yes. Sometimes I forget how generous I am. (He deals the cards.)

BLANCHE (to FELIX): Now you have a quarter of an hour of boredom ahead.

FELIX: These are the most beautiful quarter-of-an-hours of my life, Mademoiselle Blanche, the ones I spend beside you.

CORDEN: What have you got there?

BOURSEY: An ace.

CORDEN: Good. I pass.

BOURSEY: What?

CORDEN: You don't want me to trump you, do you?

BOURSEY: Don't you know what I mean when I say an ace? I mean a two. (Everybody laughs.) I don't see what's funny about that.

DANNE: You two haven't got your sign system worked out properly. When I have an ace, I press my lips together like this, and I open my nostrils like this. It always works.

LEONIDA: So that's what you're getting at when you make faces. Oh, we forgot the kitty. Blanche, bring the kitty over.

BLANCHE (*holding out an earthenware pot to each of the players in turn*):   One franc, please.

DANNE (*putting in his franc*):   It's ruinous, this game.

BLANCHE (*testing the weight of the pot*):   The pot is getting nice and heavy.

FELIX: And what about the other three, all full up?

DANNE: So they should be full up, after a whole year.

BOURSEY: I don't want to boast, but I think that was a pretty good idea of mine.

CORDEN: What do you mean? It was my idea.

BOURSEY: Excuse me. You may have suggested that we start a kitty. . . .

CORDEN: I may have? I did.

BOURSEY: But you wanted to open it every Saturday and spend the proceeds on wine.

DANNE: That would have been good.

BOURSEY: Do you think my house is a bar?

CORDEN: I didn't say anything about bars. What I said was—

LEONIDA: That wouldn't have been fair to the ladies. We don't drink, except occasionally. We would have been the ones to suffer, as usual.

BOURSEY: That's why I decided to enlarge your idea, by letting the funds add up for an entire year. And now we have a real sum of money to spend; it may be as much as two hundred francs.

EVERYBODY: Oh!

BOURSEY: Two hundred francs, I say. Perhaps more: we shall soon know. At nine-thirty the year is up and the kitty is to be counted. Now, suppose we do have two hundred francs . . .

DANNE: What a celebration!

BOURSEY: We can do something really worth while. We'll hold a dinner that will make the last Firemen's Banquet look like a snack.

LEONIDA: Let's get on with the game. I have three—

BOURSEY: I am sorry that Penuri, our wise and worthy tax collector—

PENURI (*looking up from his paper*):   Me?

BOURSEY: —did not see fit to join us and pay his contributions.

PENURI: Gambling is an immoral practice for a man who holds public office.

FELIX: I'm the public notary, and I don't see anything immoral in a friendly game.

BLANCHE: And how about Father? He's commander of the fire brigade.

PENURI: That's different. Your father is not, properly speaking, a public official.

BOURSEY (standing up): What am I then? I think I've done enough for my country not to be insulted by a mere tax collector.

PENURI: I'm not insulting—

BOURSEY: I should think not. People forget too easily that I am the one who presented the community with its only fire pump.

DANNE: Yes, but it's never been used. It's going rusty.

BOURSEY: It's not my fault if there are no fires. What am I supposed to do—go around the village setting fires right and left, just so that my pump can be used?

LEONIDA (banging the table): Are we playing or are we not? I have three—

BOURSEY (sitting down): I was waiting for you to call.

DANNE: Well, she's obviously got something good there, so I pass.

CORDEN: So do I.

BOURSEY: So do I.

LEONIDA: How's that? (She lays her cards on the table.)

BOURSEY: Good enough.

LEONIDA: Another four francs. Thank you, gentlemen. (She scoops up the money.)

BLANCHE (getting up and going to the door): Look what's arrived. Two special deliveries from Paris. One for you, Auntie. And one for Monsieur Danne.

LEONIDA: For me? Thank you. (She looks at the writing on the envelope, turns red, and puts it away hastily.)

BOURSEY: Who's it from?

LEONIDA: Oh, nobody special. My dressmaker in Paris. I'll read it later. Er—whose turn?

BOURSEY: A special delivery from your dressmaker?

LEONIDA: She's always anxious to let me know about her new styles.

DANNE (having put on his glasses): Ah, it's from my boy. He's written to tell me how he's doing at that school of agriculture. He told me he wanted to be a photographer. But I gave him a clout that knocked all those ideas out of his head. "You're going to be a farmer," I said, "like your father, and his father. Because a farmer is—"

BOURSEY: Yes we know all that. Let's get on with the game.

DANNE: Wait till I read this letter from my boy.

BOURSEY: Oh, no.

CORDEN: Not again.

DANNE (*reading*):   "My dear Dad, I am writing to tell you that they are very satisfied with me here. I've been promoted to the cowshed. . . ."

BOURSEY: The rest of us don't want to hear these intimate details about cowsheds. Read to yourself.

DANNE: If I read aloud, it's not for your benefit. It's for mine. You're not supposed to be listening. If I don't read aloud, how can I understand what I'm reading? (*Continues to read noisily.*) ". . . to the cowshed. They gave me my own sick cow to look after. . . ."

BOURSEY: Looks as if we have to wait until he's finished.

DANNE: "She is very sick. She doesn't drink. She doesn't eat. She coughs and sneezes all the time." Poor beast. She's caught a cold. "They say here that she may not last. . . ." (*Deeply moved, he passes the letter to* BOURSEY.) Read it for me. I can't see the words. My eyes are too wet. Poor creature.

BOURSEY: Courage. Don't get upset. She isn't dead yet. (*Reading.*) "As for me, I'm all right." There, you see, he's all right. He says so.

DANNE: Yes, but the cow . . .

BOURSEY: "We have been ploughing every morning. They are ploughing me to death. They want to get the seeds planted, but it won't stop raining. Still, as the proverb says:

> When February's wetter
> The dunghill is better . . . ."

DANNE: He's got it the wrong way round:

> The dunghill is better
> When February's wetter.

It's true, though. And I'll tell you why—

CORDEN: Finish it off quickly, Boursey, or we'll never get through this hand.

BOURSEY: Here comes the end. "Love and affection and best wishes from your respectful son, and will you please send my monthly allowance as soon as possible. Sylvain."

EVERYBODY: At last.

LEONIDA: Where did we get to?

BLANCHE: Father, it's nine-thirty.

CORDEN: Time to count the kitty.

DANNE: Pass.

CORDEN: Pass.

BOURSEY: Pass.

LEONIDA: Pass.

BOURSEY: That tooth is murdering me. Blanche, collect the last contributions.

BLANCHE (*going around with the earthenware pot*):   One franc each, please.

DANNE: Ruinous, this game.

BLANCHE: What's this you've given me, a foreign coin? Oh, no, it's a button.

DANNE: Excuse me, a mistake. Here you are. One franc.

BOURSEY: Now let's burn the cards.

DANNE: Don't get reckless. Some of them still have corners.

LEONIDA: Excuse me. I'm just going out to read this letter from my dressmaker. (*Exit.*)

BOURSEY: Now, gentlemen. We will proceed to the counting of the kitty.

CORDEN: The sooner the better.

BOURSEY: Blanche, bring me your workbasket. (*She empties out her workbasket on a table, and brings it to him, with a small hammer.*) And Blanche, bring in the other three pots of money.

FELIX: I'll help you. They may be heavy. (*He and* BLANCHE *go out together.*)

BOURSEY (*taking the hammer*):   There is only one way I know to open these pots and that is to break them.

DANNE: Don't break them. You might be able to use them. Let me have them. I'll find a way to get the money out without breaking them.

BOURSEY: I wish I knew what to do about this tooth.

CORDEN: Break the pots.

BOURSEY: In a moment. (*Puts the pot and the basket down and holds his jaw.*)

DANNE: I'll tell you what to do about that tooth. First you take a live mole, no more than three to three-and-a-half months old—

BOURSEY: How do you recognize a mole that's three-and-a-half months old?

DANNE: It takes practice.

PENURI: I'll tell you what's better. You take a mouthful of milk. And you keep it in your mouth all night. You don't swallow it.

BOURSEY: What if I fall asleep?

PENURI: That's all right. Fall asleep if you like. But don't swallow the milk.

CORDEN: As a professional, licensed pharmacist, may I offer a suggestion?

PENURI: A pharmacist is not a dentist.

CORDEN: Why waste money on a dentist? Do you remember how I operated on the colonel two years ago? That was a beautiful extraction.

BOURSEY: Was it easy?

CORDEN: Easy.

BOURSEY: Did it hurt?

CORDEN: How could it hurt? It was scientific. I tied a string around his tooth and attached it to the tail of a donkey. I fired one round of my service revolver, which I keep loaded for these occasions. The animal leaped forward and the tooth came from its socket like the bullet from my revolver. The colonel has never stopped thanking me since. I can do the same for you.

BOURSEY: I'll think about it. The tooth has stopped aching now. Let's get back to the kitty. (*Picking up the hammer.*) One, two, three. (*He smashes the pot.*)

DANNE: Look at all those francs.

BOURSEY: Let's get down to it. Stack them in twenties. (*They begin to count.*)

CORDEN: Three, four, five . . .

DANNE: Six, seven, eight . . .

BOURSEY: Nine, ten . . . No, what am I talking about? You're putting me off.

DANNE: I didn't say a word.

BOURSEY: You said, "Seven, eight," and that made me say, "nine, ten." Can't you count to yourself?

DANNE: No.

BOURSEY: Now I don't know where I am.

PENURI: Nor do I.

CORDEN: Let's start again. Four, five . . .

DANNE: Six, seven, eight . . .

BOURSEY: Nine, ten. No, we're doing it again. I know what. We'll all go to different corners of the room, and— (*seeing* BLANCHE *and* FELIX *coming back with the pots*) I have a better idea. You take a pot for yourself, Danne old man, and go into my bedroom with it. Corden and Penuri, you can take a pot each into my study; one of you use the desk, the other one the table. And I'll stay here.

PENURI: And we'll all come back in here afterwards for the grand total.

EVERYBODY: Yes.

CHORUS (*they sing*):

Since it's growing rather late,
And the pots are here to smash,
Let us end this one-year wait
And proceed to count the cash.

(DANNE *goes out on the left,* CORDEN *and* PENURI *on the right, each carrying his pot of money.* BOURSEY *sits down again.*)

BOURSEY: Two, four, six . . .
BLANCHE (*to* FELIX):   Ask him now, while he's alone.
FELIX: Perhaps I should wait until he's not so busy.
BLANCHE: You've already put it off for three days.
FELIX: He's had that toothache for three days.
BLANCHE: He feels better today.
BOURSEY: Money, money, money. (*Gurgling with delight.*) That makes the first hundred.
BLANCHE: Now. While he's laughing. Quick.
FELIX: I haven't thought out what to say. . . .
BLANCHE: Be brave. Just ask him. Don't waste time thinking.
FELIX: I wanted to lead up to it slowly.
BLANCHE: No, be direct. Take him by surprise. "Please, may I marry your daughter?" Isn't that simple?
FELIX: Yes. (*She pats his hand and goes out.*) No. I wish I could stop shaking. It's ridiculous. A proposal. What could be easier? (*Bracing himself.*) Sir. He didn't hear me. Sir. Monsieur Boursey.
BOURSEY: Twelve, thirteen. What is it?
FELIX: You will be able to tell, by the emotion in my voice—
BOURSEY: Every time you speak to me I lose count.
FELIX: You'd just reached thirteen.
BOURSEY: That's it. Thirteen, fourteen, fifteen.
FELIX: —by the emotion in my voice, as I say. . . . What *was* I going to say? Try again. In the three months during which I have known your daughter . . .
BOURSEY: Why don't you give me a hand? It'll go quicker.
FELIX: With pleasure.
BOURSEY: In stacks of twenty.
FELIX: In those three wonderful months, I have come to experience . . .
BOURSEY: Start counting.
FELIX (*taking a load of coins*):   Two, three . . . to experience a feeling that can only be called . . .
BOURSEY: One, two . . .

FELIX: Six, seven . . . that can only be called love. And
I would therefore like . . .
BOURSEY: Three, four . . .
FELIX: Eight, nine . . . to ask for her hand . . . Ten,
eleven . . .
BOURSEY: Seven, eight . . .
FELIX: —for her hand, twelve, thirteen, fourteen . . .
in marriage . . .
BOURSEY: Look at that. A button. That's the second one
I've found.
FELIX (*louder*): I humbly ask for your daughter's hand.
BOURSEY: Just a minute. Eighteen, nineteen, twenty. An-
other pile. They're really adding up. (*Starting to count again.*)
One, two, three . . . My dear Felix . . . four, five, six . . .
I understand the honor you do me in making this proposal.
FELIX: Thank you, sir, thank you.
BOURSEY: Where was I?
FELIX: Six.
BOURSEY: Oh, yes. Six, seven, eight . . . And I promise to
consider it carefully. . . . Another button. Somebody's been
filling up the kitty with them. Do we know any tailors?
FELIX: It wasn't me, sir.
BOURSEY: Nine, ten . . . Marriage, my boy, has its joy
and its sweetness. It also has its responsibilities. . . .
FELIX: I know. All my live I have believed in . . .
BOURSEY: Now, what have we got? (*He points to the piles
of coins.*)
FELIX: I have my practice. Nothing extraordinary at pres-
ent, but in the future . . .
BOURSEY: Five here and three there. Eight. Eight twen-
ties: one hundred and sixty.
FELIX: It might go as high as forty-five thousand.
BOURSEY: Forty-five thousand. What? Where? (*Irritably.*)
This is no good, Felix. I'm talking kitties and you're talking
dowries. (*Piling the money into the basket.*) I'm going into
the kitchen to count in peace.
FELIX: At least, may I hope that—
BOURSEY (*going out right*): You can hope for whatever
you like—as long as my daughter loves you. If I catch the
man who put all those buttons in the kitty . . . (*Exit.*)
FELIX: She does love me. She told me so. Before I even
asked her. I'll tell her the old boy said yes. (*He runs out.*
LEONIDA *comes in, carrying the letter.*)
LEONIDA: When I read the first line I almost passed out.
It's happened. He's found somebody for me. I have to be
in Paris tomorrow evening at eight o'clock. Do I dare to?

Yes, I must. It may be a question of my future happiness. If only I knew what to do and how to go. If only my mother were still alive. She would have known how to advise me. She would have said—she would have said: Go. So I shall go. But suppose they get suspicious? And that's not all. How can I travel all that way by myself? I wonder if my brother would come with me. I'll have to tell him. No, I daren't. What shall I do? I must confide in somebody. (*Enter* BLANCHE.)

BLANCHE: Oh, Aunt Leonida, you don't know how happy I am.

LEONIDA: What right have you to be happy at a serious time like this?

BLANCHE: Felix has just asked Father if I can marry him, and Father said that he can hope.

LEONIDA: What? Are you in love with Felix?

BLANCHE: I suppose I must be, otherwise I wouldn't want to marry him.

LEONIDA: That's interesting.

BLANCHE: Why?

LEONIDA: He has fair hair.

BLANCHE: What's wrong with that?

LEONIDA: And so have you. That means that you will lead a peaceful life, with no problems and no upsets, a calm life, like two sheep grazing in the same field.

BLANCHE: Sheep! Let me tell you that Felix is a charming and intelligent boy. He just had a marvelous idea.

LEONIDA: To marry you?

BLANCHE: To spend the kitty on a ball. We could invite the whole village.

LEONIDA: That would be delightful. But when, did you say?

BLANCHE: Tomorrow. Do you know what tomorrow is? Mardi Gras.

LEONIDA: Tomorrow, oh. Of course, a ball would be quite pleasant. But I have another suggestion for spending the kitty. Not quite as exciting as a ball, but more useful perhaps.

BLANCHE: What could be more useful than a ball?

LEONIDA: Suppose we all went to Paris for the day?

BLANCHE: But what good would that do?

LEONIDA: We could look in the shops. You're getting married, and you'll want to start thinking about china and curtain fabrics and nightgowns and so on. You could look for your trousseau, without *saying* so, of course.

BLANCHE: So I could. How clever you are, Aunt Leonida.

LEONIDA: Yes. You'll have to speak to your father about it. Don't tell him exactly why you want to go.

BLANCHE: Mardi Gras in Paris. Perfect. Here he is. Let me speak to him. (BOURSEY *comes in.*)

BOURSEY: All counted up. What a total! It makes the blood rush to my head.

BLANCHE: Father, you don't look very well.

LEONIDA: He looks fine.

BOURSEY: Of course I do. Wait till I tell you how much we have here.

BLANCHE: That toothache must be painful.

BOURSEY: I'd forgotten all about it.

BLANCHE: Your cheek is all swollen.

LEONIDA: I can't see it.

BOURSEY: Now you mention it, it is beginning to throb again.

BLANCHE: Poor Father. Does it hurt very much?

BOURSEY: It does now.

BLANCHE: If I were you . . .

BOURSEY: You'd put a live mole aged three to three-and-a-half months in your mouth. The trouble is, how do you tell the age of a mole?

BLANCHE: No. If I were you I'd go to a dentist.

BOURSEY: There isn't one in the village.

BLANCHE: There are plenty in Paris. The best dentists in the world.

LEONIDA (*aside*): She's not as sheepish as she looks.

BOURSEY: Don't joke with me. Go all the way to Paris for the sake of a tooth?

BLANCHE: Two little tiny hours by train.

BOURSEY: But the expense.

BLANCHE: You could do it for nothing.

BOURSEY: How?

BLANCHE: You could pay all the expenses from the kitty. We could all go.

BOURSEY: So we could. We could all go, and we could spend the kitty in Paris.

BLANCHE: You could have your tooth pulled out, we could look around the shops . . .

LEONIDA: I could keep my appoint—

BOURSEY: Your what?

LEONIDA: We could visit the monuments.

BOURSEY: Yes. The Panthéon, the Tower of Saint Jacques, the Champs Élysées . . .

BLANCHE: The Louvre, the Eiffel Tower, the Concorde . . .

LEONIDA: The Tuileries, the Luxembourg Gardens . . .

BOURSEY: The Follies . . .
BLANCHE: But wait. Suppose the others don't want to go?
BOURSEY: They will have to be convinced. Leave that to me.

(CORDEN, DANNE, PENURI *and* FELIX *return.*)

PENURI: Gentlemen, here is the total of the portion of the kitty that was placed in my jurisdiction. Upon counting and rechecking the result I find that my portion comes to one hundred and thirty-one francs. I must add, however, since we are interested in complete totals, that I have found a number of buttons, namely five, among the coins.
CORDEN: So have I.
BOURSEY: And I.
BLANCHE (*looking at* DANNE):   Buttons, eh?
DANNE: Somebody must have made a mistake.
CORDEN: I have one hundred and twenty-eight francs and four buttons.
BOURSEY: I have one hundred and five francs. And nine buttons.
DANNE: I have one hundred and twenty-seven francs.
BOURSEY: And no buttons?
DANNE: No buttons.
BOURSEY: That's strange.
PENURI (*who has written down the totals*):   That, gentlemen, gives us an over-all total of four hundred and ninety-one francs.
EVERYBODY: Ah!
PENURI: Plus eighteen buttons.
BOURSEY: A very nice kitty.
CORDEN: Magnificent.
DANNE: I thought it would be bigger.
CORDEN: So it would have been—without the buttons.
BOURSEY: And now, gentlemen, the great moment has come when we must deliberate and vote on how the kitty shall be spent.
EVERYBODY: Yes, yes! (*They sit around the table in the center.*)
FELIX (*appearing at the back*):   Have you counted it up?
BOURSEY: Yes, we have. Come in. We need your vote. We are all good friends, gentlemen, and even if our votes diverge, we still respect each other's opinions. Who wants to speak first?

CORDEN ⎫
DANNE ⎬ (*standing up together*):   I do!

BOURSEY: I can see that we are full of suggestions this evening. Which one of you asked first?

CORDEN ⎫ I did!
DANNE ⎭

BOURSEY: This is becoming difficult.

PENURI: The custom in deliberative assemblies is for the younger man to give way in favor of the older.

BOURSEY: That solves it. Corden, you have the floor. . . .

CORDEN: Thank you. But I believe that Danne is older than I am.

DANNE: I am not. I've always been younger than you, much younger, as long as I remember.

CORDEN: It's not true. I refuse to speak first.

BOURSEY: Gentlemen, gentlemen, I was counting on a brilliant discussion, with flashing remarks from man to man, from friend to friend. And all I hear is petty squabbling.

CORDEN (*standing up*):   Very well. I'll speak first. Not because I'm the oldest, but because I am the most reasonable.

PENURI: Good for you.

CORDEN: I shall be brief. . . .

BOURSEY (*graciously*):   That's a pity.

CORDEN: Thank you. Here we are with this considerable and unexpected sum of money. We must spend it in a manner worthy of our positions; we are, after all, not unimportant men in this village. I therefore propose that we write to my friend Chevet and order a large turkey, stuffed with truffles. (*Murmurs of disagreement.*)

BOURSEY (*shaking a little bell*):   Ladies, gentlemen. Please. We shall listen to everybody's suggestion in turn . . . even the most stupid ones.

CORDEN: Eh?

LEONIDA: I'm against truffles. I don't like them.

BLANCHE: Nor do I.

BOURSEY: They also happen to upset my stomach.

DANNE: I prefer mushrooms. Fried.

CORDEN: I'm sticking to truffles.

BOURSEY: Right. Next opinion. Danne?

DANNE: The weather is fine and my old buggy is big enough for all of us. Let's go to Cressy and spend the day at the fair.

EVERYBODY: No, no. Terrible idea. Waste of time. Ridiculous . . . etc.

BOURSEY (*ringing his bell*):   Order, order. One at a time.

CORDEN: I still think that a fat turkey, overflowing with truffles . . .

DANNE: You didn't let me tell you about the fair. You see the sideshows, the snakes, the magicians, the donkeys with two heads, and the fat woman. She's really something to see. And sometimes they let you touch her. It's fun, that is.

FELIX: Excuse me, I have a much better suggestion. . . .

BLANCHE (*in a hiss*):   Don't talk about the ball. It's all been changed. We have something else.

FELIX: Oh, it's changed?

BOURSEY: All right, Felix. Go ahead.

FELIX: I—um—er—I need a few more minutes to think.

PENURI: Although I have not contributed to the kitty, perhaps you will allow me to give you an outside, objective view. I have a proposal which, I am sure, will please everybody. If you don't wish to hear it, just say so, but you'll be sorry if you neglect this valuable and unifying motion.

BOURSEY: Go ahead, Monsieur Penuri, for God's sake.

PENURI: The most desirable attribute in woman is maidenly virtue. Ladies and gentlemen, virtue is on the decline. We must revive it, encourage it.

DANNE: What's that got to do with us?

PENURI: Why not hold a carnival, and select the most virtuous girl in the village of Endives-Under-Glass to be the queen of the carnival?

CORDEN: How can you tell who is the most virtuous girl?

PENURI: That would be up to the judges.

CORDEN: Who are the judges?

PENURI: We are.

CORDEN: Much easier to buy a turkey, a thumping great turkey swamped with truffles, and have done with it.

DANNE: Or drive to the fair in my buggy and spend a whole day with the fat lady and the snakes and—

BOURSEY: Order. Silence. This is my house, so I shall speak last. I claim all your attention.

BLANCHE: Good old Daddy.

BOURSEY: Ladies and gentlemen, Paris is the capital of the world. It has the finest dentists in the world. . . .

PENURI ⎫
DANNE ⎬   What?
CORDEN ⎭

BOURSEY: I mean it is the center of the arts, industry, and entertainment. Paris has everything. I therefore propose that we take the excursion train tomorrow to Paris.

BLANCHE 〕
LEONIDA 〕 Bravo!

DANNE: No good. I've been to Paris before. I passed through it forty-one years ago on the way to Lille.

CORDEN: An excursion? But we'll have no money left for eating. I would have thought that a giant turkey, brimming with truffles . . .

BOURSEY: But truffles don't agree with the rest of us. They make us ill.

CORDEN: Paris will make me ill.

BOURSEY: But if the majority decides on Paris . . .

CORDEN: The majority would never—

BOURSEY: We'll see. Let's proceed to the vote.

EVERYBODY: The vote. The vote.

PENURI: Shall I, as the only impartial member of this assembly, take charge of the ballot box?

BOURSEY: Yes. Good idea. (*He hands out a sheet of paper to each person.*) The ballot box. (*He gives* PENURI *a hat.*)

PENURI: One, two, three, write. (*Everybody except* BLANCHE *and* PENURI *writes.*) No crossings-out or you spoil your ballot paper. Has everybody decided? The ballot is closed. (*He takes the papers and puts them in the hat. To* LEONIDA.) Now we will count the votes. (*He takes out the papers one at a time.*) One turkey with truffles . . .

CORDEN: Hooray.

PENURI: Silence, please. Paris. (*Cheers from* FELIX, BOURSEY, LEONIDA *and* BLANCHE.) Paris. (*More cheers.*) The fair at Cressy.

DANNE: Hooray, very good, terrific, that's for me.

PENURI: And the final vote is for Paris. (*More cheers.*) Total number of votes: five. Votes for Paris: three. An absolute majority for Paris.

CORDEN: I suppose we'll be able to get a decent meal there.

DANNE: We can go to the cattle market and the slaughter-houses. I have a cousin who works in one of the slaughter-houses. He'll show us round.

BOURSEY: There's one other thing: we certainly won't spend the whole of our four hundred and ninety-one francs on the fare. We'll have something left over for our personal needs, such as visiting dentists and so on.

DANNE: That reminds me: I could do with a new pickax.

CORDEN: I've just thought of something too, foolish perhaps, but—

BOURSEY: What is it?

CORDEN: Nothing, nothing. (*Aside.*) It may be a question of my future happiness.

LEONIDA (*aside*):   I'll be able to keep my appointment.

BOURSEY: Let's all have an early night. We'll have to catch the five twenty-five tomorrow morning.

BLANCHE (*to* FELIX):   How are you going to get up?

FELIX: I won't sleep. I'll be too excited thinking about you.

CHORUS (*they sing*):
>   What a lucky group are we—
>   Off to Paris in the train.
>   One whole day to stay and see
>   All the sights upon the Seine.

ACT II

(Paris. A large, elegant restaurant.)

BENJAMIN *(arranging a table)*: Is that a customer? At this time of the morning?

SYLVAIN *(entering hesitantly)*: No, it frightens me. It's too luxurious.

BENJAMIN: May I help you, monsieur? What are you looking for?

SYLVAIN: Some information. Last night I was at the Casino and I met a young lady who calls herself Miranda the Sensitive.

BENJAMIN: I know her.

SYLVAIN: Good. Then she really exists. I was beginning to wonder after those drinks last night. She told me to meet her here for lunch.

BENJAMIN: At this time of the morning?

SYLVAIN: No, a bit later. But I wanted to know beforehand if it's possible for the two of us to eat lunch in a private booth for seventeen francs. That's all I have.

BENJAMIN: Seventeen francs—well, we could certainly give you something.

SYLVAIN: I don't just mean rolls and coffee. I'm entertaining a young lady, don't forget.

BENJAMIN: I could do you a nice sheep's cheek in vinegar.

SYLVAIN: Sounds appetizing.

BENJAMIN: Or a steak—rather thin, rather narrow, but a steak. Or an omelette made with one egg.

SYLVAIN: Perfect. We shall also want dessert. Something unpretentious. At an unpretentious price.

BENJAMIN: How about stewed prunes?

SYLVAIN: You're joking.

BENJAMIN: Or a strawberry tart?

SYLVAIN: Fresh?

BENJAMIN: This week's.

SYLVAIN: Plenty of crust?
BENJAMIN: Acres.
SYLVAIN: Plenty of strawberries?
BENJAMIN: Dozens.
SYLVAIN: Put two strawberry tarts aside. (*Takes out a cigar case.*) Have a cigar.
BENJAMIN: Thank you, monsieur. Oh no, this is the cabbage-leaf type. I only smoke Havanas.
SYLVAIN: So do I, when I can afford them. But my father doesn't allow me enough to buy more than one Havana a month.
BENJAMIN: A tightwad, eh?
SYLVAIN: He's the finest of men, my father. But a peasant, after all. He has a farm at Endives-Under-Glass, and he thinks he can turn me into a farmer too.
BENJAMIN: It's a noble profession.
SYLVAIN: Yes, but too earthy for my taste. I wanted to be a photographer, and specialize in girls . . . you know: models, standing under waterfalls or kissing trees. But Dad wouldn't hear of it. He sent me to this school at Grignon.
BENJAMIN: To learn farming?
SYLVAIN: Yes, but I don't know a cauliflower from a carrot. As soon as I got there they stuck me in the cowshed, and in twenty-four hours they had me carting manure all over the place. Two days later I left . . . without telling Dad, of course.
BENJAMIN: Suppose he finds out?
SYLVAIN: That's where I've been smart. I write to him every month. I go back to Grignon to post the letter and pick up my monthly allowance: one hundred francs.
BENJAMIN: A hundred francs—that's rough.
SYLVAIN: It is after the first few days. From the fifth of the month on I'm always in debt. I wish I knew some way to earn a little on the side. Something not too strenuous. Tell me, what do you make a month at this job?
BENJAMIN: Depends on the tips. About three hundred on the average.
SYLVAIN: That would do me nicely. I wouldn't be ashamed to wait in a café.
BENJAMIN (*coldly*):   There's nothing to be ashamed of.
SYLVAIN: It would suit me. Always in the money. Tips. Plenty of women around,
BENJAMIN (*persuading himself*):   And it's very satisfying work. Creative.
SYLVAIN: I bet. What's your name?
BENJAMIN: Benjamin.

SYLVAIN: Good for you. Listen, Ben, if you hear of an opening for a bright young man, keep me in mind, will you?

BENJAMIN: Certainly.

SYLVAIN: And you'll save me a booth for lunch?

BENJAMIN: Number four, monsieur. By the window, facing onto the boulevard.

SYLVAIN: Perfect. If I'm not here when Miranda arrives, tell her to wait on one of those chairs. I don't want her to start spending before I get here.

BENJAMIN: Very good, monsieur. Don't worry about it.

SYLVAIN: Thanks, Ben. You're a pal. Come and have a coffee with us at lunch time.

BENJAMIN: Thank you, monsieur. (SYLVAIN *goes out.*) He called me Ben! That's the kind of person I like: no swank, even though he comes from a good family.

(*Noises from outside. Sounds of running feet. Shouts of "Stop thief, stop thief." Another waiter comes in.*)

SECOND WAITER: Did you see that? A pickpocket. He got away.

BENJAMIN: Where?

SECOND WAITER: Right outside the restaurant. He tore off around the corner.

BENJAMIN: Did you see him?

SECOND WAITER: No. He snatched somebody's watch and disappeared.

BENJAMIN: It doesn't pay to carry a watch these days.

(SECOND WAITER *goes out. Enter* BOURSEY, DANNE, COR-DEN, LEONIDA, *and* BLANCHE.)

DANNE: First time I ever saw a thief close up. He looked just like anybody else. Talk about exciting. I'm glad we came to Paris, after all. It's a good beginning to the day.

LEONIDA: I've never seen anybody run at that speed before.

BOURSEY: He went right by me. If I'd reached out I could have touched him.

CORDEN: It was your duty to stop him.

BOURSEY: I'm safer minding my own business. We didn't come to Paris to catch crooks. Interfere with a man like that and he might give you a nasty knock. (*Noticing* BENJAMIN.) Waiter!

BENJAMIN: Monsieur?

BOURSEY: How's your food?

BENJAMIN: Very good, monsieur.
DANNE: Bring some in. I'm starving.
BENJAMIN: Now?
DANNE: Yes. Immediately now.
BENJAMIN: Would you like a booth, gentlemen?
LEONIDA (*going to the nearest table*):   We would not.
Booths are for loose women.
BOURSEY: That told him.
BENJAMIN: Don't get annoyed, ladies. Sit where you
like. I'll bring you a menu. (*Aside.*) People who are hungry
before lunch. . . . Must come from the backwoods.

(*He goes off.* BOURSEY *lays his umbrella on another table.*
CORDEN *and* LEONIDA *put their overnight bags, and packets
wrapped in brown paper, on other tables.* DANNE *has a bun-
dle tied up in a red, spotted handkerchief, which he puts in
the middle of the table at which they are sitting.*)

BOURSEY: That's the way. Unload your stuff.
DANNE: Don't worry, I will. I brought my old shoes to
change into. (*He puts them on.*)
BOURSEY: We'll make this restaurant our headquarters.
If the lunch is good and cheap, we'll come back for dinner.
BLANCHE: Can you imagine Felix missing the train like
that after he promised me he wouldn't oversleep?
BOURSEY: Lawyers. They're not used to getting up before
the afternoon.
LEONIDA: I'm tired. Let's sit down. (*She and* BLANCHE *do
so.*)
BOURSEY: Don't get too comfortable. We're only staying
for a bite. We want to see all the sights and there isn't too
much time.
CORDEN: Whose fault is that? The first sight we saw this
morning was the dentist's waiting room.
BOURSEY: Corden, I don't wish you any harm. But if you
ever break a leg, I shall consider it my duty to go to the
doctor with you, and to see that your pain is relieved as
soon as possible.
DANNE: How does your tooth feel now?
BOURSEY: Fine. First he started to play about with my
gum. That didn't help. Then he tugged the tooth out in one
clean movement. I forgot to tell you: it was only ten
francs. . . .
CORDEN: Very cheap.
BOURSEY: . . . So I took the money from the kitty.
CORDEN: Ten francs. I could have done it for three, with
a donkey.

BENJAMIN (*re-entering*): The menu.
BOURSEY (*taking it*): That's my decision.
CORDEN: It's everybody's decision.
BOURSEY: If you're going to keep questioning my authority, I'm going home.
BLANCHE: Father . . .
LEONIDA: Gentlemen . . .
CORDEN: I didn't say a thing.
DANNE: Don't start fighting in public. We ought to explain to this man (*he indicates* BENJAMIN) that we're in Paris to enjoy ourselves. We want to eat like kings.
BOURSEY: Nothing but the best.
DANNE: We have a lump sum to get rid of—found money, you might say.
BENJAMIN (*aside*): I don't like it. Who are these people?
BOURSEY: Advise us.
BENJAMIN: I have some juicy mutton chops with—
BOURSEY: No, no mutton.
CORDEN: We eat it every day.
DANNE: I sell it.
BENJAMIN: Or some Chateaubriand steaks . . .
CORDEN: No, no steak.
BOURSEY: Let me explain the situation. We don't want beef, mutton, veal, chicken, duck, or goose.
DANNE: Nor do we want potatoes, cabbages, beans, or peas.
BENJAMIN: Let me think. How about a slice of canteloupe melon for the ladies?
BLANCHE: Yes. I love melon.
LEONIDA: So do I. I adore it.
BENJAMIN: Two slices?
BOURSEY: Just a minute. Let's check the price. (*To* DANNE *and* CORDEN.) You can't trust these city waiters. "Melon, per slice, one franc."
CORDEN: In February, off season? That's dirt cheap.
DANNE: They're giving it away.
BOURSEY (*to* BENJAMIN): Melon for everybody.
BENJAMIN: Five slices of canteloupe. (*Writes it down.*)
BOURSEY: Make it ten slices.
BENJAMIN: And what to follow?
CORDEN (*taking the menu*): "Pâté de Nerac."
DANNE: I don't know what it is, but I like the sound of that.
CORDEN: So do I.
BOURSEY: How much is it?
CORDEN: Two francs.

BOURSEY: That's not dear.

DANNE: They're giving it away.

BOURSEY (*confidentially, to the others*):   I always seem to land up in the right places. I have a nose for them. (*To* BENJAMIN.) That Nerac business—bring a large helping for everybody.

BENJAMIN: Five pâtés. And what could you like for entrée?

BOURSEY: An entrée too? Well, why not? The prices are so reasonable. Have you got something delicate and unusual?

DANNE: This is a special occasion.

CORDEN: It says here that they have tournedos à la plenipotentiary.

(*They all crowd round the menu.*)

LEONIDA: What is it made of?

BENJAMIN: It's a new dish. A chef's special. Hunks of stag meat with minced quail, strained anchovies, olives, marinated oysters, lettuce, and truffles.

CORDEN: Truffles. That's for me.

DANNE: And me.

EVERYBODY: And me.

BOURSEY: Tournedos à la plenipotentiary for everybody. Well done.

LEONIDA: And something sweet for the ladies.

BLANCHE: Oh yes.

DANNE: And some Roquefort cheese. Strong enough to make me sit up.

BOURSEY: What have you got in the way of dessert?

BENJAMIN: I can offer you a floating palace à la Radetzki or a froufrou à la Pompadour.

BOURSEY (*to* BLANCHE):   Which do you prefer?

BLANCHE: You choose for me.

CORDEN: The floating palace must be light—if it floats. (*They laugh.*)

BOURSEY (*to* BENJAMIN):   We'll take the lightest floating palace you have. (*More laughs.*)

CORDEN: The balloon variety. (*Hysterical laughter.*)

(DANNE *slaps* BENJAMIN *on the back.*)

BENJAMIN (*aside*):   Comedians, comedians. (*Aloud.*) It's rather early. The chef will need about half an hour to prepare the dishes.

BOURSEY: That's all right. We'll leave our things and stroll around the Concorde and up the Champs Élysées.

BLANCHE: Or along the Rue de Rivoli to look at the shops.

LEONIDA (*to* BOURSEY):   Stay here with me, Theodore. I have something to tell you. It's important.

BOURSEY: But I want to see the Concorde and the—

LEONIDA: Please. It's a matter of life and—

BOURSEY: All right, all right. (*To* BLANCHE.) Your aunt is a little tired. I'll stay here with her. You others go off by yourselves.

CORDEN: I have an errand. There's something I want to buy near here.

DANNE: Don't you worry, Blanche. We'll go off together and have a good time on our own, eh? (*He digs her in the ribs.*)

CHORUS (*they sing*):

First $\begin{Bmatrix} \text{we'll} \\ \text{you'll} \end{Bmatrix}$ look in all the stores
All along the street.
Then $\begin{Bmatrix} \text{we'll} \\ \text{you'll} \end{Bmatrix}$ hurry back in force,
Just in time to eat.

(DANNE *gives his arm to* BLANCHE. CORDEN *goes out by himself.*)

BOURSEY: Now then. About this matter of life and—

LEONIDA: Yes. I don't know how to tell you.

BOURSEY: You left your handbag in the train? I'm not buying you another one.

LEONIDA: No, it's not that. Theodore, you are my brother, my only friend, the only person I can trust. Promise you won't be angry with me.

BOURSEY: For what?

LEONIDA: Promise first.

BOURSEY: Not till I know what I'm promising.

LEONIDA: Theodore, I have been wicked.

BOURSEY: You? You've never been wicked in your life. You wouldn't know how to be.

LEONIDA: I should have asked your permission.

BOURSEY: I wouldn't have given it.

LEONIDA: That young lady you've been reading about for four years in the paper, in the advertisement . . .

BOURSEY: The one who wants a modest home in a small, well-situated town?

LEONIDA: Yes.

BOURSEY: What about her?

LEONIDA: Theodore, I—

BOURSEY: So that's it. So that's how you've been spending your money. Well, it wasn't a bad idea. Except that it didn't work.

LEONIDA: But it has worked. Read this letter. I received it yesterday at home.

BOURSEY: From your dressmaker.

LEONIDA: I'm sorry I lied to you. I was embarrassed. (*Gives him the letter.*)

BOURSEY: It's signed X. Who is X?

LEONIDA: It's Monsieur Poche, a marriage broker.

BOURSEY: The cattle-monger!

LEONIDA: Not cattle, Theodore, please.

BOURSEY: "Mademoiselle, come to Paris as soon as you can. I have just the man for you. A gentleman in a high position, dark, gay, good-looking. I have arranged to introduce you to him at my salon tomorrow night at eight o'clock. . . ."

LEONIDA: That's tonight.

BOURSEY: "Be on time, and bring some of the family with you for him to meet. The address is 55 Rue Joubert. . . ." We'll have to let him know we're in Paris.

LEONIDA: I've already done it. I couldn't sleep last night, so I sent him a telegram.

BOURSEY: There was no need for that. Minimum price for a telegram is three francs. A letter would have been enough.

LEONIDA: Theodore, can I count on you to come with me?

BOURSEY: Of course you can. Don't I want your happiness as much as I want my own?

LEONIDA: What shall we do about Corden and Danne?

BOURSEY: We'll take them with us. We won't tell them why. They can be the rest of the family.

LEONIDA: I'm so glad you're not angry. (*Kisses him.*) I've been a burden to you for too long.

BOURSEY: A burden? Not at all. But naturally I'm glad you'll be going off on your own. It'll be good for you. You've been turning a bit sour in the last few years.

LEONIDA: I like that. You should talk. I've never met such an impossible person to live with. I can tell you frankly that if this hadn't happened now—

BOURSEY: Shush. Here comes somebody.

(*Enter* SYLVAIN.)

SYLVAIN: Miranda must be here by now.

BOURSEY } Sylvain!
LEONIDA }

SYLVAIN: Oh. (*Forcing a smile.*) Monsieur Boursey, Mademoiselle Leonida, what a treat to meet you in Paris.

BOURSEY: Yes. Your father is with us.

SYLVAIN: Really? It must be my lucky day.

BOURSEY: Yes, he's out looking at the shops with Blanche. But he'll be back shortly.

SYLVAIN: Here?

BOURSEY: Yes, for lunch.

SYLVAIN: Well, if he's visiting the shops, why don't I go out and look for him? (*He starts to go out and sees* BLANCHE *and* DANNE *coming in.*) Trapped.

DANNE: Here we are again. I bought a brand new pickax. You don't know how I've dreamed about having a new pickax.

BLANCHE: I can think of nothing more charming than walking along the Champs Élysées with a man who is swinging a pickax.

SYLVAIN (*aside*): Better make the best of this. (*Coming forward.*) Hello, Dad.

DANNE: My boy. (*Embraces him with a kiss on both cheeks.*) Well, son, how is she?

SYLVAIN: Who's that?

DANNE: Your poor old cow.

SYLVAIN: It's kind of you to remember. She's still bad.

LEONIDA (*to* BOURSEY): Have you made a note of all the gifts we have to deliver in Paris?

BOURSEY: Yes. I'll never do any favors again. Somebody gave me an old boot here to take somewhere. I think I'll dump it under the table and forget about it.

DANNE: How is it you're not at the school?

SYLVAIN: I decided to . . . that is, I was sent . . . You see, the cow is sick, so they asked me to take it to the doctor at Alfort.

DANNE: They put you in charge of it?

SYLVAIN: Yes.

DANNE: My boy! I always knew you had a great future. So they have cow-doctors nowadays. Well, well.

SYLVAIN: I stopped off in Paris on the way back. Lucky I met you. While we're here you might as well give me next month's allowance. You'll save the postage.

DANNE: Good idea. (*Takes out his wallet.*) Wait a minute, though. You're on your own here. You might lose it.

SYLVAIN: Of course I won't.

DANNE: You stay with us for the day, son, and I'll give it to you this evening, before you leave for Grignon.

BOURSEY: That reminds me. We all have an invitation for this evening.

DANNE: Where?

BOURSEY: A delightful evening, music, pastries, punch . . . with a friend of mine. (*To* LEONIDA.) What's his name again?

LEONIDA: Poche.

BOURSEY: Poche. Dear old Poche, one of my oldest and dearest friends. He's in the match business.

BLANCHE: Will there be any dancing?

BOURSEY: Certainly. All the time. This is a big evening.

BLANCHE: I have no evening dress.

BOURSEY: It's informal.

DANNE: I can leave my pickax in the cloakroom. Is it all right if my boy comes along?

BOURSEY: With pleasure. It'll add to the family—to the company.

SYLVAIN: I'd be glad to come, Dad, but—

DANNE: You're coming. No arguments. I want you to learn how to behave with high-class people. (*Puts his pickax on a nearby table.*) I'll give you your money when we leave there.

SYLVAIN: What's the address?

LEONIDA: 55 Rue Joubert. Ask for Monsieur Poche.

SYLVAIN: I'll be there. Dad, I'll see you—

LEONIDA: Don't keep talking, Sylvain. We have to sort out the gifts. Get the bags onto the tables.

(*They empty their overnight bags and parcels on the tables.*)

BOURSEY: Well, this is a nice load to get rid of. Rings, bracelets, fans, letters . . . we must have brought the whole countryside with us. How can we deliver all these gifts in one day?

BENJAMIN: I wonder what they're up to with those parcels. (*Goes closer.*)

BOURSEY: The first thing to do is to share it out equally.

BENJAMIN: Sharing it out, eh? I'll have to watch this. (*Goes even closer. Voice from a distant table: "Waiter, waiter."*) Oh, damn! Coming!

(*Enter* CORDEN, *puffing and red in the face, looking as if he has a pillow under his shirt.*)

CORDEN: Whew. Hope I didn't keep you waiting. Hello, Sylvain. (SYLVAIN *nods to him gloomily.*)

LEONIDA: You look as if you haven't stopped running since you left.

CORDEN: I was in a hurry.

BOURSEY: What's wrong with your chest?

CORDEN: Does it show?

BOURSEY: You're all puffed up like a pigeon. It looks as if your stomach has moved up to your neck.

CORDEN: I was going to tell you: I've been embarrassed by my stomach for some time; it has a tendency to sag. So I thought: while we're in Paris I might as well get a good thick belt to hold it up.

BLANCHE: A corset.

CORDEN: A health belt. So I bought one. Out of the kitty.

EVERYBODY: Shame. A disgrace. Out of our money, etc.

BOURSEY: It hasn't done you any good. You had a fat belly; now you've got a fat chest. Squeeze the belt a bit tighter and you'll have a fat head.

CORDEN: The salesman told me it looked fine, but it's doing wicked things to my ribs.

BENJAMIN: Luncheon is served.

EVERYBODY: Good. At last. I'm famished, etc.

DANNE (*to* SYLVAIN): Sit down and have a bite with us, son.

SYLVAIN: I've eaten, thank you. (*Aside.*) Miranda isn't here yet. (*Aloud.*) I'll see you later.

DANNE: Stay here. Look at all this food. (*Holding* SYLVAIN'*s arm.*) Have a chair.

BENJAMIN: Here's a chair. (*To* SYLVAIN.) I've found a job at The Smiling Bull.

SYLVAIN: Tell me afterwards. Thank you, waiter.

BOURSEY: What a fragrant melon!

LEONIDA: Delicious.

DANNE: Only one franc a slice.

CORDEN: I'll never live to enjoy it. My belt is crushing me.

DANNE: What do you think of my new pickax, son?

SYLVAIN: Very beautiful.

DANNE: Look at it. I bet they haven't got any pickaxes like that at your school, eh?

SYLVAIN: Nothing quite that ferocious. They have a few small ones.

DANNE: Are you growing many beetroots down there?

SYLVAIN: Not too many—a beetroot here, a beetroot there.

DANNE: You can't beat beetroots. But you have to give them plenty of dung, tons of it.

CORDEN: I can see some truffles. Pass me a few.

DANNE: And how about turnips? Are you growing turnips?

SYLVAIN: Oh yes. We're very big on turnips. Turnips wherever you look.

BOURSEY: Is he ever going to stop with his vegetables?

DANNE: Can't beat turnips. They're like parsnips. You have to give them plenty of dung. Pile it on.

CORDEN: Hurry up with those truffles. I wish I could take this belt off.

DANNE: And carrots. Are you growing many carrots?

SYLVAIN: The place is alive with them. I've grown thousands myself. They're my specialty.

DANNE: Good for you. You can't beat carrots. But you have to smother 'em in dung.

BOURSEY: You and your dung. Do you have to keep talking about it while we're eating?

DANNE: If it wasn't for dung you wouldn't be eating at all. Right, Son?

SYLVAIN: Yes, Dad.

DANNE: You see? My boy says so, and he's a farmer, like me.

LEONIDA: But at table . . .

DANNE: No good being soft-mouthed about it. Everything you eat—bread, meat, red radishes, white turnips, green cucumbers—where does it all come from, hey?

EVERYBODY: From dung.

BOURSEY: Now shut up about it. You've wrecked my appetite.

BLANCHE }
LEONIDA }   And mine.

CORDEN: Not mine. I'm still waiting for the truffles.

DANNE: Tell me, Son. Do you kill many pigs down there?

BOURSEY: Here we go again.

DANNE: Show me how you go about killing a pig, a real fat porker.

SYLVAIN (*looking round uneasily*):   I just—kill it.

DANNE: There's a right way and a wrong way. You roll your sleeves up like this. You take the animal's head in this hand . . .

EVERYBODY: Go home! Dry up! Give us a break! It's disgusting, etc.

SYLVAIN (*standing up*):   Well, I'll push off.

DANNE: Where are you going?

SYLVAIN: Back to Alfort to see how the cow is. I'll see you later.

DANNE (*holding him back*): Have a glass of wine first.

SYLVAIN: Thanks, I don't want one now.

DANNE: Drink up, Son. It's good for the shoulders. (*Gives* SYLVAIN *a glass of wine.* SYLVAIN *drinks it.*) That's better, isn't it? Straightened you out, didn't it?

SYLVAIN: Yes, thanks. Good-by for now, everybody. See you later. (*Aside.*) I'll come back when they've finished.

DANNE: You can get your money this evening, Son.

SYLVAIN: I'll be there. Fifty-five Rue Joubert. Ask for Poche. (*Exit.*)

DANNE: He's a good boy. Do anything for me. Loves the soil.

BOURSEY: Has everybody finished? We don't want to spend all day in here. Waiter, the bill.

BENJAMIN: Right away, monsieur.

LEONIDA: First we'll get rid of the gifts.

CORDEN: Then we'll take a look at the Arch of Triumph.

BENJAMIN: Your bill, monsieur.

BOURSEY: Now then . . . here, what's this? Four hundred and fifty-two francs? Where did that come from?

EVERYBODY: What? Four hundred and fifty-two francs? Impossible, etc.

BOURSEY (*to* BENJAMIN, *who is bringing in glasses of liqueurs*): What are those?

BENJAMIN: Liqueurs.

BOURSEY: Take them away.

CORDEN: We didn't order any liqueurs.

BENJAMIN: They're on the house. You don't pay for them.

BOURSEY: Take them away. Four hundred and fifty-two francs. Where does that come from? You thought to yourself, "Out-of-towners," didn't you? "I'll take them for everything they've got."

BENJAMIN: But monsieur . . .

BOURSEY: We can be as smart as you, you know.

BENJAMIN: The prices are all written on the menu.

BOURSEY: Give me a menu.

BENJAMIN: With pleasure, monsieur. (*Brings one over.*)

BOURSEY (*snatching it*): You see: melon—one franc per slice.

DANNE: It says ten francs on the bill. Swindle!

BENJAMIN: It is ten francs, monsieur. You can't see the zero because of the frame on the menu.

EVERYBODY: Oh!

CORDEN: But look at this pâté de Nerac. Two francs a portion.

BENJAMIN (*taking the menu back*): Twenty francs, monsieur. The frame is hiding the zero again.

EVERYBODY (*peering over*): Oh!

LEONIDA: We've been robbed.

DANNE: All the zeroes are hidden.

BOURSEY: I refuse to pay. Where is the manager?

BENJAMIN: In the other dining room over there. If you'd like to discuss it with him . . .

BOURSEY: I certainly would. Let's go.

EVERYBODY (*they sing*): Let's go.

> Someone's trying to cheat us
> When we're in the right.
> We won't let them beat us.
> We'll go out and fight.

(BOURSEY, DANNE, LEONIDA *and* BLANCHE *troop out.* CORDEN *is still sitting.*)

CORDEN: I don't like to argue about meals, especially when my stomach feels as if it's two-thirds of the way up my body. I ought to go out and get some fresh air; it might make a difference. I keep thinking about that advertisement. I wrote to the newspaper. They told me to apply to a fellow named Poche, at 55 Rue Joubert. I could nip over and see him, and meet the others later. Who knows?—it may be a question of my future happiness. Walter!

BENJAMIN: Monsieur?

CORDEN: Is Rue Joubert far from here?

BENJAMIN: No, monsieur. You go out of the door, turn right, and it's the second on the right.

CORDEN: Thank you. When my companions return, will you tell them I'll meet them on top of the Arch of Triumph in one hour?

BENJAMIN: Yes sir.

CORDEN: Happiness, here I come. (*He goes out. Noise of a violent argument from the next room.*)

BENJAMIN: They're battling away like wild animals. Anybody'd think they hadn't ordered the most expensive dishes on the menu.

(BOURSEY *comes in, followed by the others.*)

BOURSEY (*shouting back*): Call anybody you like. I'm not paying.

DANNE: I'd rather go to court.

SECOND WAITER (*going out left*): A policeman? Yes, boss, there's one outside.

BOURSEY: Bring the entire police force, for all I care.

BLANCHE: Father, they may . . .

BOURSEY: They can't do a thing. I laugh in their faces. Ha, ha, ha.

LEONIDA: I thought they'd at least reduce the bill. And all they tell us is that the liqueurs were free.

DANNE: It's a mockery. We didn't even drink them.

BENJAMIN: Monsieur, the other gentleman told me to tell you that . . .

BOURSEY: You again? Get out of my sight. (BENJAMIN *leaves.*) Collect your things, everybody, as if we're going to walk out. Then they'll have to give way.

(*They pick up their parcels.* DANNE *takes his pickax and* BOURSEY *his umbrella. The* SECOND WAITER *comes back with a* POLICEMAN.)

SECOND WAITER: There they are. They wouldn't pay.

BOURSEY: You mean we wouldn't let ourselves be swindled.

LEONIDA: Melon at ten francs a slice!

DANNE: Ten slices. That's a hundred francs. Did you ever hear of anything like it?

POLICEMAN: Let me see the menu.

(BENJAMIN *gives it to him.*)

BOURSEY: Some menu. It's full of hiding places and secret zeroes. Can you see what they've done with that frame around the edges? (*He gesticulates with his umbrella. A watch falls out of it.*)

POLICEMAN: What's that?

EVERYBODY: A watch.

POLICEMAN: Who owns it?

BOURSEY: It's not mine.

EVERYBODY: Nor mine.

POLICEMAN: The chain is broken or cut. This watch has been stolen. How did it get inside your umbrella?

BOURSEY: I didn't put it there. You can't tell the time from a watch that's inside an umbrella.

BENJAMIN (*to* POLICEMAN): Search them. They've got all kinds of loot in their parcels and pockets.

POLICEMAN: So you don't know where the watch came from and you refuse to pay your bill. You'd better come along with me, all four of you, to the station.

DANNE: What station?
POLICEMAN: The police station. (*To* BENJAMIN.) And
bring your menu. They'll pay you there.
BLANCHE: What are they going to do to us?
BOURSEY: Don't be afraid, my child. An honest man is
never afraid to be judged by the law of his country. Follow
me.

(*Chorus*):

LEONIDA BLANCHE DANNE BOURSEY	Take us to the station. Let the law decide If their accusation Has been justified.
BENJAMIN SECOND WAITER	Drag them to the station. Tie them up inside, Under observation Till they can be tried.
POLICEMAN:	Come down to the station. Do not try to hide From investigation If you haven't lied.

(*They all go out, except the* SECOND WAITER.)

SECOND WAITER: Jailbirds, the lot of them. I bet they're
a gang.

(FELIX *enters hastily and sits at a table.*)

FELIX: Waiter, bring me a steak. Rare. I'm in a hurry.
SECOND WAITER: Right away, monsieur.
FELIX: I had to take a later train. Where can they have
got to? I've already been to the Panthéon and the Tower
of Saint-Jacques. After I've eaten I'll try the Concorde and
the Champs Élysées.
SYLVAIN (*entering*):   They've gone at last. I wonder if
Miranda—
FELIX: Sylvain!
SYLVAIN: Hello, Felix. You weren't with the others, then?
FELIX: Have you seen them?
SYLVAIN: They were here a few minutes ago.

FELIX: Blanche too? (SYLVAIN *nods.*) Where are they now? Which way did they go?

SYLVAIN: I have no idea.

FELIX: Damn!

SECOND WAITER: Your steak, sir. It's very rare.

FELIX: Rare? It's raw.

SYLVAIN: Waiter—oh, you're not the same one. Have you seen a young lady here? She's expecting me.

SECOND WAITER: A very highly dressed lady, monsieur? Yes, she's in booth four. She's already had thirty francs worth of drinks.

SYLVAIN: Thirty francs? Is she having an alcohol rub?

WAITER (*as a woman's voice calls:* "*Waiter*"): There she is again. She's waiting for her melon.

SYLVAIN: Melon! Thirty francs worth of drinks! I'd better get away. Tell her I've been ordered to sit on a jury . . . for two weeks. (*He rushes out. The woman's voice is heard again, calling the* WAITER.)

FELIX: Waiter, bring me some bread.

SECOND WAITER: Bread for number five. Melon for number four. Coming, coming! (*He hurries off.*)

ACT III

(Waiting room in a police station. A table, a chair, a bench, and a police-station quartet: BOURSEY, BLANCHE, LEONIDA, and DANNE, who are shown in by the POLICEMAN. They line up and sing, to a Mozartean melody.)

CHORUS:

>Gloom without measure.
>Happiness foiled.
>This day of pleasure
>Has now been spoiled ...
>This day of pleasure
>Has now been spoiled.

POLICEMAN: Wait here, please. I'll call Monsieur Chute.

BOURSEY: Chute, who's he?

POLICEMAN: The assistant police commissioner. He'll want to question you. *(Exit.)*

(They put their parcels on the table.)

DANNE: What are we going to say when they question us?

BOURSEY: Stop waving your pickax. You'll stick somebody with it.

(DANNE puts his pickax in a corner.)

LEONIDA: Do you think they'll torture us?

BOURSEY: Keep calm. It's all a misunderstanding.

LEONIDA: Perhaps so, but here we are in prison.

BOURSEY: We are not in prison. We are in the police station. People walk into the police station every day. And walk out again.

DANNE: If you'd listened to me we'd be in Cressy now, at the fair, with the snakes and Siamese twins and fat women. It's your fault.

112

BOURSEY: That's it—blame me. How could I know that they stuff watches in your umbrella in Paris?

DANNE: Who told you to bring your umbrella?

BOURSEY: Corden told me, that's who. (*Turning.*) Corden, it's your— Where is he?

DANNE: I haven't seen him since we left the restaurant.

BLANCHE
LEONIDA   } Neither have I.

BOURSEY: Trust him to scuttle away at the first sign of danger.

DANNE: He probably hid under a table.

BLANCHE: At least, he is free.

BOURSEY: I would not exchange my chains for his liberty.

BLANCHE: Chains? I hope they don't lock us up.

BOURSEY: Leave it to me. I'll handle this man myself. He's only an assistant, isn't he? I'll talk to him confidentially. I'll make myself known.

DANNE: I'll tell him all about the kitty.

LEONIDA: I'll explain that we came to Paris to see the sights.

BLANCHE: And the shops.

BOURSEY: Now listen to me, all of you. If the four of us talk at once, we're lost. One firm, clear voice must speak for us all.

DANNE: We need a lawyer.

BLANCHE: I wish Felix were here.

BOURSEY: What we need is a calm, eloquent, quietly persuasive man. Luckily, we have such a man at our disposal—with us. . . .

DANNE: Thank you.

BOURSEY: I venture to say that you will find all these qualities in me.

BLANCHE: Yes, let Father speak for us.

DANNE: Good enough. Don't be nervous. I'll be right behind you.

BOURSEY: Quiet, here he comes.

(*Enter* CHUTE.)

CHUTE: Ah, there are four of you.

DANNE: For the time being.

CHUTE: Sit down, won't you? (*Goes to the desk and consults some papers.*)

BOURSEY: You are too kind, Commissioner. We thank you from the bottom of our innocent hearts. (*They sit on the bench.* BOURSEY *speaks to the others in an undertone.*) Keep

calm. Smile freely, like people who have nothing to fear.
(*They all smile.*) Very good. Stay like that.

CHUTE (*looking up*): It appears that a watch was discovered in an umbrella belonging to one of you. Why are
you all grinning at me like that?

BOURSEY: To show that our consciences are easy.

CHUTE: Tell me about the watch.

BOURSEY (*standing up*): In the life of every man, Commissioner, as in the life of every country, there are moments
of crisis, when—

CHUTE: Very likely. Now explain about the watch.

BOURSEY: Before going into the murky details of this
affair, which could sully the lives of an entire family, I think
it is my duty as a man, as a father, as a citizen, to proclaim
my respect for the law of this country. I am proud to be—

CHUTE: Will you please answer my question?

DANNE: Your Worship, he's telling the truth.

CHUTE: All right, let's hear your version. Take off your
hat.

DANNE: Thank you, Your Worship; it doesn't trouble
me.

CHUTE (*to* BOURSEY): You sit down.

DANNE: You see, we wouldn't be here, except for the
kitty. We caught the five twenty-five this morning . . .

BLANCHE: And Felix must have overslept . . .

CHUTE: About the watch . . .

BOURSEY (*standing up*): Commissioner, if you will allow
me . . .

CHUTE: Sit down. (DANNE *and* BOURSEY *sit down.*) No,
not you (*to* DANNE). Carry on with what you were saying.
Stand up, man.

DANNE: I said we should have gone to the fair at Cressy.
With the fat woman, and so on. But the others voted against
it.

CHUTE: Let's get this straight. You came to Paris this
morning.

BOURSEY (*standing up*): From Endives-Under-Glass.

CHUTE: Sit down. (BOURSEY *and* DANNE *sit.*) You came
to see the sights . . .

DANNE (*standing up*): It was the kitty.

BOURSEY (*standing up*): We came here, Commissioner, to
admire the great city of Paris.

CHUTE (*to* BOURSEY): All right, if you insist on talking.
(*To* DANNE.) Sit down. (*They both sit down.*) Not you (*to*
BOURSEY). Stand up again. (*To* DANNE.) And take off your
hat. Now, you were saying?

BOURSEY: I wasn't saying a thing. He (*pointing to* DANNE) was talking.

CHUTE: Let's start again. How did this stolen watch get into your umbrella?

BOURSEY: As commander of the Endives-Under-Glass fire brigade, invested with the full responsibility of that onerous position . . .

DANNE: He gave the community a fire pump.

BOURSEY: I think I have always done my duty for my country. . . .

DANNE: As a farmer and the son of a farmer—

LEONIDA: I'm afraid we don't know anything about the watch.

CHUTE: Now we're getting to it.

BLANCHE (*standing up*): We haven't done anything wrong.

LEONIDA (*standing up*): Our lives have been pure and stainless.

CHUTE: That's enough. Sit down.

BOURSEY (*standing up*): Look into my past. It will answer for my future.

CHUTE: Silence. Sit down, all of you. Listen to me. I'm sure that you're harmless, the lot of you. There is no charge against you. You can go.

EVERYBODY: Hooray. We're free. No charge, etc.

(LEONIDA, BLANCHE, *and* BOURSEY *stand up joyfully.* DANNE, *who is on the end of the bench, goes down with it.*)

CHUTE: But be careful. The authorities are watching you. (*He rings a bell and sits down again.*)

BOURSEY: I told you we'd be safe if you trusted in me. (*To* DANNE.) Why did you talk so much? You nearly got us into trouble.

CHUTE: Oh, I forgot. There is a witness. (POLICEMAN *enters.*) Bring in the waiter. (*Enter* BENJAMIN.) What have you got to say?

BENJAMIN: Nothing. All I want is for them to settle the bill.

CHUTE: What bill?

BENJAMIN: Their lunch bill. They wouldn't pay it. (*He hands the bill to* CHUTE.)

BOURSEY: Four hundred and fifty-two francs—never!

DANNE: We're not paying for all those zeroes around the edges.

CHUTE: Let me see: melon, pâté, tournedos a là plenipotentiary; this is an expensive meal. Why did you refuse to pay?

BOURSEY: Because we were not aware . . .

DANNE: They tried to swindle us. They're thieves.

BENJAMIN: There may be thieves in this room, but I'm not one of them.

EVERYBODY: What?

CHUTE: What do you mean by that? You'd better explain yourself.

BOURSEY: Yes, you'd better.

BENJAMIN: It's true. If the police ever look in your bags and parcels, they'll see what you are.

BOURSEY: Our parcels?

DANNE: What's he getting at?

CHUTE (*opening the bags and parcels*):   Rings, bracelets, fans . . . Where did all this come from?

LEONIDA: They are gifts for us to deliver.

DANNE: Which proves that we're honest folk who can be trusted with other people's belongings.

BENJAMIN: Some honest folk.

DANNE: Why, you table-clearing, plate-washing, young— (*he starts toward* BENJAMIN. *A chisel falls out of his overcoat pocket.*)

POLICEMAN (*picking it up and handing it to* CHUTE):   A chisel.

DANNE: It's mine.

CHUTE: A burglar's tool.

BOURSEY: I bet you bought that out of the kitty too.

DANNE: Of course I did. That's what the kitty was for.

CHUTE (*he speaks to the* POLICEMAN. *Then*):   In your own interests, I think we'd better get you to give a sworn testimony.

BOURSEY: I think I've done enough for my country. It's not my fault if we never had a fire.

DANNE: We're honest folk.

BLANCHE: We haven't done anything wrong.

CHUTE: That's enough. Follow the policeman outside, the ladies too. I'll call you back when I want you.

POLICEMAN: Outside, all of you. Hurry up. (*They go out slowly, protesting.*)

DANNE: Stop pushing. (*Exit.*)

CHUTE: Now then, tell me everything you know. At what time did they go into your restaurant?

BENJAMIN: It was barely nine o'clock. I was sweeping out when I heard somebody on the boulevard shouting: "Stop, thief."

CHUTE (*taking notes*): Go on.

BENJAMIN: These people came rushing in. They looked frightened to me. They ordered lunch, all the best dishes on the menu, and they said they had plenty of money. "Found money," they said.

CHUTE: That's serious. Go on.

BENJAMIN: Some of them went out while the dishes were being prepared. That stout woman stayed behind with the leader of the gang. She told him she had committed a fault. I was listening. When the others came back they emptied the loot out on the table . . . jewelry, fans, rings. They shared it out, and the leader of the gang said: "This is a nice load to get rid of."

CHUTE: Yes, it all ties up. Go on.

BENJAMIN: One of them came in later than the others, a fat one. The policeman didn't get a chance to pinch him. He got away. He had something under his jacket. I couldn't see what it was. It made him all bloated. It must have been a sack, at least.

CHUTE: More plunder. Yes. Go on.

BENJAMIN: Well, after they'd eaten their fill, they refused to pay. That's it.

CHUTE: I see. Well, you can go now. You'll be called as a witness.

BENJAMIN: What about my bill?

CHUTE: You'll be paid at the registrar's office. Go out that way. (BENJAMIN *goes out of another door.* CHUTE *rings.* POLICEMAN *reappears.*) Bring those people in again.

POLICEMAN (*at the threshold*): Back in here. Get a move on.

(BOURSEY, LEONIDA, BLANCHE, *and* DANNE *re-enter.*)

EVERYBODY: It's a disgrace. Honest folk like us. Shame, horror, etc.

BOURSEY: I protest, in the name of civilization.

CHUTE: About what?

BOURSEY: They emptied our pockets.

LEONIDA: They confiscated all our property.

BOURSEY: Our money, our watches, our parcels. All they left us was our handkerchiefs.

DANNE: And who needs them?

BOURSEY: It's an affront to our rights.

CHUTE (*standing up*): Enough of these fine words. I know you now. You're one of those gangs who descend on Paris during festivals. You wait till the evening comes, then you roll drunks and snatch purses.

EVERYBODY: Roll what? Do what? Snatch what? etc.

DANNE: Your Worship. As a farmer and the son of a farmer . . .

CHUTE: You can stop playing yokels now. I know what you are. I've just sent for a cart to take you all to prison.

EVERYBODY: To prison!

CHUTE: You're a gang of pickpockets. (*He goes out.*)

LEONIDA: What is a pickpocket?

BOURSEY: It's a kind of tailor. Um—after a suit is finished . . .

BLANCHE: It means a thief.

BOURSEY: Impossible! We're not thieves.

DANNE: They're going to put us in prison.

BOURSEY: That's what he said. We're in trouble now. Oh, injustice!

(*They hear the double door being closed on them outside.*)

BLANCHE: We're locked in.

LEONIDA: And Monsieur Poche will be waiting for us this evening. My happiness is destroyed. My future is ruined.

BLANCHE: Felix won't want to marry me now.

DANNE: Sylvain won't find us this evening. I'll have to send his money by mail. More expense.

BOURSEY: My friends, are you ready to risk everything in one great enterprise?

EVERYBODY: Well? What is it? What do you mean? etc.

BOURSEY: Speak low. I am going to propose a course of action that may live in the annals of historic endeavor. . . . Don't be afraid. You all remember the fate of the Count of Monte Cristo. He was imprisoned in the Bastille because the king's mistress hated him. He stayed there for thirty-five years.

BLANCHE: Thirty-five years!

DANNE: I thought that was Robinson Crusoe.

LEONIDA: No, it was Latude.

BOURSEY: Latude, what are you talking about? Now, I think of it, though, it was Latude. Forget about Monte Cristo. Now, what I propose is that we escape. What do you say to that?

DANNE: Just let me out. But how?

BLANCHE: The door is locked from the outside.

BOURSEY (*tiptoeing across the room*):   But there is still a window. (*They rush across after him.*) Hush! Not a murmur. Don't let them hear.

LEONIDA: But the ladies . . . how about us?

BOURSEY: We are only one flight up. Below is a court-yard, and I can see a pile of . . .

DANNE: Manure! There it is. Nice and soft to land on. Like a featherbed.

LEONIDA: But how about this evening? We won't be able to go out like that, smelling . . .

BOURSEY: Ah, look what I've discovered. A rope.

EVERYBODY: A rope! How lucky! Just what we need! Etc.

BOURSEY: I'll go out first. You wait here. I'll bring a ladder, and it'll be easy for the rest of you. (*He seizes the rope. There is a clanging outside.*) Oh God, it's on the end of a bell. (*Sound of bolts being drawn outside.*) Keep calm. Keep smiling.

(*They sit down on the bench.* DANNE *looks at it fearfully, then sits at* CHUTE's *desk.* POLICEMAN *enters. They all smile at him.*)

POLICEMAN: Who rang that?

DANNE: That what?

POLICEMAN: That bell.

BOURSEY: Somebody in the courtyard outside.

POLICEMAN: Don't be impatient. The van will be here soon. (*He goes to the window, pulls a bar across it, and padlocks the bar in place.*)

DANNE: Look at the size of that padlock.

BOURSEY (*rummaging in his pockets*): And not a thing left to bribe him with. Excuse me, Inspector. They've taken away all my money, but if you ever happen to be passing through or near Endives-Under-Glass, my house and table are at your disposal.

POLICEMAN: What do you mean?

BOURSEY: Come and have dinner with us. And I'll make you a handsome present.

POLICEMAN: Oho! Attempted bribery, eh? *That'll* be something to add to the evidence. (*Exit.*)

LEONIDA: You made it worse.

BOURSEY: I was trying to—

DANNE: Wait. They've forgotten something. My pickax.

BOURSEY: Why couldn't they have forgotten something that would be useful to us?

DANNE: But it is. My lovely new pickax. It's all sharp and pointed. I'll dig a hole in the wall and we can walk out through the next house.

EVERYBODY: Wonderful. Better than the window. Easy, etc.

BOURSEY: Get down to it. (DANNE *lifts his pickax.*) No, stop. They'll hear you. It's no use.

LEONIDA: What can we do?

DANNE: Why don't you all sing? Sing as loud as you can. Drown me and the pickax.

BLANCHE: What songs do we know?

LEONIDA: There's my aria from *The Barber of Seville.* (*Singing.*) "*Una voce poco fa . . .*"

BOURSEY: No, it's loud, but not noisy enough. Do you remember that song I wrote for the firemen's banquet? "A tired old man"? (LEONIDA *and* BLANCHE *nod.*) Good. Off you go. (*To* DANNE.) Wait till the first line, then start banging. Now, put plenty of expression into it. (DANNE *swings his pickax.*)

CHORUS:

> A tired old man
> Once knocked on my door.
> His clothes were so dirty
> He must have been poor.
>
> So dirty, so dirty,
> His clothes were so dirty,
> His trousers and shirt, he
> Just must have been poor.

(*At the end of the chorus some lumps of plaster fall away.*)

DANNE: I forgot about that. What are we going to do with the plaster?

BOURSEY: In our pockets, quick. (*They pick up the debris and put it in their pockets.*) Right, second verse.

CHORUS:

> But where could we put him
> To lie down and rest?
> Except in the cellar—
> Yes, that would be best.
> The cellar, the cellar,
> Away in the cellar . . .

(*The door bolts grind open.*)

BOURSEY: They're coming. What can we do about the hole? How can we hide it?

DANNE: We can't. We're finished.

BOURSEY: Leonida! You stand in front of it. There.

DANNE: Good. She's just wide enough.

BOURSEY: Don't move an inch. Smile!

(CHUTE *comes in. They all smile at him.*)

CHUTE: I forgot to take your names for the testimony. You first.

BOURSEY: Theodore Athanasia Boursey, of Endives-Under-Glass, commander of the—

CHUTE: Don't start that again. The young lady?

BLANCHE: Blanche Rosalie Boursey.

CHUTE: And you?

DANNE (*standing with his pickax behind his back*): Leonard Robert Danne.

CHUTE (*to* BOURSEY): Is this lady (*pointing to* LEONIDA) your wife?

LEONIDA (*coming forward*): No, I am his sister. I am unmarried.

BOURSEY: Don't move!

CHUTE: Come here. I'm not going to bite you.

LEONIDA: I'm comfortable here.

CHUTE: Come forward. (LEONIDA *approaches him slowly.* DANNE *swiftly takes her place in front of the hole.*) Now, what is your name?

LEONIDA: Zelmira Leonida Boursey.

CHUTE: That's all. We're having some trouble finding a cart. It's Mardi Gras, all the vehicles are out. But we'll have one here soon. (*He goes out with the* POLICEMAN.)

DANNE: Back to work. Keep singing.

BOURSEY: Second verse again.

CHORUS: But where could we put him
To lie down and rest?
Except in the cellar.
Yes, that would be best.

The cellar, the cellar,
Away in the cellar . . .

DANNE: That's enough. The hole's gone through.

LEONIDA: Saved!

BOURSEY: Quiet now.

DANNE: I'll see where we've got to. Pooh! Stinks of tobacco. (*Reappearing hurriedly.*) We're finished. It's the policemen's lounge. There are three of them in there.

BOURSEY: Quick. Try and fill up the hole again before they come back.

POLICEMAN (*entering*): Transport's ready. We commandeered a taxi. Hurry, before you get up to more mischief. What's this? A hole in the wall? Who did that?

DANNE: The mice.

POLICEMAN: A pickax, eh? Attempted escape, eh? Now you're really in the juice. (*Blows a whistle. Two other* POLICEMEN *enter.*)

POLICEMEN:
>   Drop them in the clink
>   Get them under locks
>   Before they have a chance to think
>   We'll have them breaking rocks.

PRISONERS:
>   Save us from the clink
>   Spare us all the locks
>   Before we have a chance to blink
>   They'll have us breaking rocks.

ACT IV

(In Paris. The marriage salon owned and run by POCHE. *We are in the "meeting room," just off the main hall, spacious, brilliantly lit by a candelabra—altogether an atmosphere of vulgar splendor.* JOSEPH, *the servant, is skimming the woodwork with a dustcloth or encouraging the fire. Enter* POCHE.)

POCHE: Haven't you finished yet, Joseph?

JOSEPH: Almost, monsieur. Shall I see to the lights in the other room?

POCHE: The main salon. Yes, by all means. Do it now. This is a big evening. Money will flow. A young lady is coming from Endives-Under-Glass with a dowry of one hundred thousand francs. Did you order the ice cream and the pastry? Did you get the dancing partners?

JOSEPH: Yes, monsieur. They're all there, except for Anatole.

POCHE: What's happened to him?

JOSEPH: He wanted an increase. He said he won't work for less than ten francs on Mardi Gras.

POCHE: Ten francs—the robber! I offer him five francs for an easy evening's work, and I'm paying for the white gloves. It's adequate, isn't it?

JOSEPH: That's what I told him.

POCHE: I admit that he's my best man. He has an insolent manner that the ladies seem to love. He's only a hairdresser's assistant, after all, but the other night somebody took him for the English ambassador.

JOSEPH: And he smells so good.

POCHE: That's true. You always think he's just been fished out of a bottle of lavender water. That goes down well in the salon.

JOSEPH: He said he'd send one of his friends along to replace him.

POCHE: I'm sorry about this. He was my star attraction.

123

Well, never mind. For ten francs we can do without him. Put the lights on in the main salon, but nowhere else. (JOSEPH *goes out.*) Seven forty-five. If I'm not mistaken, my beautiful Leonida will be here on the dot of eight. (*Takes a note from his pocket and reads it.*) I'll just refresh myself on the list of personal particulars. "Dark, flowing hair," that's good. "Warm, golden complexion," even better. "Sad and tender temperament"—that could be a problem—"mellowed by a natural sweetness"—excellent—"docility"—I'm not sure about that—"and spontaneous good humor"—ah, she came through. "Which shines in my eyes and lights up my personality." She's a poet. "In other words, I am gay, unaffected, gentle, overwhelmingly charming and modest." She certainly knows how to make out a prospectus. "Since I was a child, my life has been devoted to my brother, a widower, who is many years my senior. He is an irritable, uncouth, surly loudmouth, and yet I have never complained of my fate, either to him or to anybody else. My soft pink lips have remained sealed, and I have cared for him with the undemanding affection of a saint." I wonder if she's religious. "If the gentleman you have found for me is suitable, I would consent to share a home with him in a small, well-situated town. . . ."

(SYLVAIN *enters.*)

SYLVAIN: Are you Poche?
POCHE: Yes. What do you want?
SYLVAIN: I've come for the evening. . . .
POCHE (*aside*): Anatole's replacement! (*Aloud.*) Wait there. I'll look you over. (*He puts his papers down.*)
SYLVAIN: What a way to treat guests.
POCHE: Now. Turn round, slowly. Not bad. I like your jacket, but your trousers could have done with another pressing. The creases should be like knives.
SYLVAIN: You know how it is. You wear what you have.
POCHE: There's a button missing from your sleeve. I don't like that.
SYLVAIN (*aside*): Next he'll want to wash behind my ears.
POCHE: Go into the dressing room. One of the girls will replace that button.
SYLVAIN (*aside*): They really take care of you here.
POCHE: I don't have to remind you that I expect impeccable behavior, chaste language—no doubtful words or smutty allusions—and a firm, upright stance. There. (*Straightens* SYLVAIN's *shoulders.*)

SYLVAIN: I know that. You have to be careful what you say to ladies.

POCHE: One other thing: you're not to touch the ice cream or the bonbons.

SYLVAIN: But I thought—

POCHE: It doesn't matter what you thought. The agreement is that you are entitled to one cake and a cup of tea during the course of the evening.

SYLVAIN: I can't stand tea. It makes me vomit.

POCHE: Vomit—that's a word I don't like. When the tray of tea is brought round, say something like: "My doctor forbids me to indulge in it." Be a man of the world. It's not so hard.

SYLVAIN: I'll try.

POCHE: Wait here. I'll get your gloves. (*He takes a pair of gloves from a table.*)

SYLVAIN: What are these for?

POCHE: Only one of them is to be worn, on your left hand. You hold the other one, and keep your right hand bare, for greeting guests. There are your five francs.

SYLVAIN: Five francs?

POCHE: No discussions, please. I've had enough trouble this evening with Anatole. Five francs for gentlemen and three for ladies; it's the standard rate.

SYLVAIN: Well, if it's the standard rate . . . (*puts the money in his pocket*). Seventeen and five—twenty-two. Good.

POCHE: What's that about twenty-two?

SYLVAIN: Just a little private arithmetic. I can afford a meal tonight.

POCHE: Tell Anatole from me that if he drops out again at such short notice, he's finished.

SYLVAIN: You keep talking about Anatole. Anatole who?

POCHE: Anatole your friend.

SYLVAIN: I don't know any Anatoles.

POCHE: Who sent you then?

SYLVAIN: My dad. He said go to 55 Rue Joubert and ask for Monsieur Poche. So here I am.

POCHE: Ah, now I understand. Your father wants me to find you a wife.

SYLVAIN: Does he?

POCHE: Obviously. I beg your pardon, monsieur. I took you for one of my . . . But now I see that you are a client.

SYLVAIN: About this wife business . . .

POCHE: So I'll trouble you for the gloves and the five francs.

SYLVAIN: You want them back? I was just getting used to

them. (POCHE *is already taking the gloves out of his hands.*
SYLVAIN *returns the money.*)

POCHE: Please have a chair. I'll sign you in the clients'
register. You'll be in company with some of the finest names
in France. (*He opens a creaking great book, after undoing
the padlock.*)

SYLVAIN: You could use a little grease on those hinges.

POCHE: May I please have your name?

SYLVAIN: You can borrow it. Sylvain Jerome Danne.

POCHE: Oh, what a name!

SYLVAIN: What's wrong with it?

POCHE: It's magnificent.

SYLVAIN: Thank you.

POCHE: Don't mention it. That will be one hundred francs
security, please.

SYLVAIN: Oh no. No security. Tell you what: with a magnificent name like mine, couldn't you give way on the hundred francs?

POCHE: Impossible. It's for the preliminary paper work.

SYLVAIN: Dad didn't say anything to me about a hundred
francs. You'd better talk to him when he comes.

POCHE: Is he coming this evening? Splendid. Then we'll
settle later.

(JOSEPH *comes in.*)

JOSEPH: Monsieur, your guests are arriving. . . .

POCHE (*closing his book and looking through a door*):
Good. The girls are here. I'll start grouping them.

SYLVAIN (*looking over his shoulder*): You can group me
with that plump one over there.

POCHE: Come with me . . .

(*He goes out, followed by* SYLVAIN.)

JOSEPH: The boss is going to be tied up this evening.
Gives me a chance to make hay with the ice cream and the
cups of tea.

CORDEN (*entering*): Very nice. Very nice. They've really
dressed it up. (*He is clad in high style.*)

JOSEPH: It's the gentleman who was here this morning.
I'll tell the boss. (*Exit.*)

CORDEN (*admiring himself in a glass*): Very impressive.
Suits me beautifully. And a perfect fit, considering it was all
hired at short notice. How are those two grease stains? Gone,
that's good. I can still smell the stain remover, though. Ben-

zine. It stinks. I drenched myself in cologne, but the benzine is winning. I should have left the stains. She might not have noticed them. Now she won't be able to get near me. Well, it's too late to retreat now. There's too much at stake. I'm dying to see her. Either she's beautiful, as she says in the advertisement, or she's ugly. If she's beautiful—happy days; I'm only a man, after all; I'm not made of marble. If she's ugly; well, I'm not so young myself, and with a dowry that large she'll be well worth my fifty francs deposit. I estimate our value this way: she has five thousand a year; add that to my four thousand from the pharmacy; that makes nine. I'll be able to set her up in a little business on the side; perfumes or ladies' underwear or tobacco, snuff and stationery—to keep her occupied. Let's be conservative and say that brings in another thousand a year: that makes ten. I'll be on a level with Boursey. I'll present the community with another pump. He'll be furious. There's only one obstacle. Poche tells me that I have a rival. The meeting was arranged for him. Still, as Poche says, may the better man win. (*Admiring himself again.*) My rival is going to have a hard time beating that. (*Sniffing.*) I only wish I could do something about that benzine. I wonder what happened to Boursey and the others. I waited for two hours on top of the Arch of Triumph; I didn't come down till the man drove me away, ten minutes after closing time. It's not very nice of them to let me down like that. I'll have a word with Boursey about it when I see him. I'll probably meet them on the last train going back tonight. (*Enter* POCHE.) Good evening. Am I late?

POCHE: Not at all. It's the young lady. I'm still waiting for her. (*Inspecting* CORDEN.) Very good. The vest is stylish.

CORDEN: Isn't it?

POCHE: But you shouldn't throw out your chest like that. You bulge.

CORDEN: It's the belt. I mean, it's natural.

POCHE: What's that curious odor?

CORDEN: I can't smell anything. Tell me, is my rival here yet?

POCHE: Yes, he's strolling about in one of the other rooms.

CORDEN: Let me see him.

POCHE: I'm afraid I can't.

CORDEN: Is he good-looking?

POCHE: Not bad.

CORDEN: Better than me?

POCHE: Well . . .

CORDEN: Confidentially.
POCHE: He is a little less—broad.
CORDEN: What does he do for a living?
POCHE: He works.
CORDEN: Has he got any medals, titles, or decorations?
POCHE: Not that I know of.
CORDEN: Then we're on a par. Don't forget that you promised to let me have first crack at the lady.
POCHE: Rest assured. (*Looking at his watch.*) I hope she doesn't let me down.

(JOSEPH *comes in with a tray of ice cream and pastry.*)

JOSEPH: Monsieur.
POCHE (*eagerly*): Has she arrived?
JOSEPH: No sir. It's Amanda. I saw her eating an ice cream and a pastry.
POCHE: The hussy. I'll give her pastry. (*To* CORDEN.) Excuse me, an important visitor has just arrived. (*He goes out.*)
CORDEN: He has a very fine clientele.
JOSEPH (*offering the tray*): Ice cream or pastry, monsieur?
CORDEN: I'll have one of each—to start with. Oh, you have three kinds of ice cream. Which smells the strongest?
JOSEPH: I beg your pardon, sir?
CORDEN (*He sniffs the flavors*): I'll take the chocolate. (*Aside.*) Now I'll look in the other rooms. I may see my rival. (*Exit.*)
JOSEPH: Just time for a quick pastry. (*He stuffs one into his mouth.*) Somebody's coming. (*He hurries out with his mouth full of pastry.*)
BOURSEY (*entering*): In here. Quick! Close the door behind you. (LEONIDA, BLANCHE, *and* DANNE *come in behind him.*) Are you sure nobody followed us?
BLANCHE: Certain. We didn't stop running.
LEONIDA: A fine way to go to a ball.
BLANCHE: Ah, a fire. (*She goes and warms herself near it.* LEONIDA *joins her.*)
BOURSEY: Free at last!
DANNE: I could do with something to eat.
BOURSEY: So could we all.
JOSEPH (*entering*): Ice cream or pastries, ladies and gentlemen?
BOURSEY: Pastries! Look at them!
DANNE: Just leave the tray here.
JOSEPH: I'm sorry, monsieur, I am not permitted to.

BOURSEY: I'll pass them around. (*He passes them, one at a time, to* DANNE, *who passes them on to* BLANCHE *and* LEONIDA, *putting a few in his pocket on the side.*) Young man (*To* JOSEPH), will you tell Monsieur Poche that the Bourseys are here from Endives-Under-Glass?

LEONIDA: Including Mademoiselle Leonida.

DANNE: And Danne the farmer, son of a farmer.

JOSEPH: With pleasure, monsieur. (*He goes to the door.*)

DANNE (*stopping him*):   You don't want to carry that heavy tray with you. Put it down here till you come back.

JOSEPH: I have to take it round the salon, monsieur. (*He goes out.*)

DANNE: Come back soon.

(CORDEN *enters.*)

CORDEN: I can't get rid of this benzine smell. It's worse than a gas leak.

BOURSEY: Corden. What are you doing here? Do you know Poche?

CORDEN: Why, I—of course I do. Known him for twenty years. An old friend.

BOURSEY: You never mentioned him to me before.

CORDEN: Don't talk to me in that tone, Boursey, after what you have on your conscience.

BOURSEY: You're hardly the one to talk about conscience.

CORDEN: Walking out on me like that, leaving me on top of the Arch of Triumph till after closing time. It was windy as hell.

DANNE: So were you as windy as hell.

BOURSEY: Skulking away at the first sign of danger.

DANNE: Hiding under tables.

CORDEN: I didn't skulk anywhere. I was waiting on top of the Arch of Triumph. . . .

BOURSEY: I'm surprised that you didn't feel ashamed at the sight of that monument dedicated to courage and honor.

CORDEN: Are you questioning my courage and honor, monsieur?

BOURSEY: I am not questioning them. I am denying them, monsieur.

CORDEN: I refuse to stomach that kind of an insult, monsieur.

BOURSEY: Take your corset off, then you'll be able to stomach anything, monsieur.

LEONIDA: Don't start quarreling now.

BLANCHE: Father, please.

DANNE: Come on, boys, shake hands. We're all children of Endives-Under-Glass, aren't we? We're friends.

BOURSEY: We were. I was not the one who broke up the friendship. I will not shake hands with a coward.

BLANCHE: Father, stop that kind of talk.

LEONIDA: Haven't we had enough trouble for one day?

BOURSEY: Very well. I yield to the persuasions of my family. (*He shakes hands with* CORDEN.)

CORDEN: Now tell me what happened to you.

BOURSEY: We were battered by the tempest of destiny. Our lives were in the balance. . . .

DANNE: It was all because of the watch and the chisel.

CORDEN: What was?

DANNE: The reason why they took us to the prison.

CORDEN: What prison? Who?

BOURSEY: All four of us, in a taxi.

DANNE: The policeman was sitting in front with the driver.

CORDEN: You were in a taxi with a policeman. . . .

BOURSEY: We had to find a way to escape.

CORDEN: From a taxi?

DANNE (*to* BOURSEY): You're muddling him up. Let me explain. (*To* CORDEN.) You see, the pickax didn't work. We went through to the policemen's lounge. And the rope didn't work either. It was on the end of a bell.

CORDEN: Yes . . .

DANNE (*to* BOURSEY): Now he understands. You can fill in the details.

BOURSEY: We drove down the boulevard in a taxi; the police cart hadn't arrived. The taxi had to go slowly because of the crowds. There was a Mardi Gras procession, with trumpets blowing as the main float went by, and the crowd shouted, "There it is, there it is." The policeman, who was sitting in front, looked out of the window to the right to see what was going on. At the same moment, on the left, four clowns who had finished in the procession made a sign to the cab driver to stop, because they thought he was free. So we got out and they got in. And the policeman was still looking out of the other window.

BLANCHE: And the traffic moved on. . . .

BOURSEY: And the four clowns went to prison with the policeman. (*They all laugh helplessly, except* CORDEN.) And we got away in the crowd.

DANNE: I'd like to have seen that policeman's face when he found the four clowns in the back. (*They laugh again.*) Now do you understand?

CORDEN: Not a word.
DANNE: It must be that belt. (*Punches him playfully in the tummy.*) Ooh, you smell terrible!
CORDEN: Just a little benzine. I'll find something to neutralize it. (*He goes out.*)
DANNE: So that's it. He drinks benzine. I always wondered. . . .
BLANCHE: That reminds me. I'm thirsty.
DANNE: So am I. Must be the pastry. Let's find that tray.
LEONIDA: You two go. Theodore and I will stay here.

(DANNE *gives* BLANCHE *his arm. They go out.*)

LEONIDA: I wonder where Monsieur Poche is.
BOURSEY: I'm very curious to meet that man.
LEONIDA: Is my hair terrible?
BOURSEY: No, but your shoes are covered with dust. It's lucky that I still have my handkerchief. (*Takes it out. A lump of plaster falls from his pocket.*) There goes a piece of the police station. (*He rubs his handkerchief over her shoes.*)
LEONIDA: Hurry, hurry. He may come in.
BOURSEY: I know that this is going to be a waste of time. I'd never have the luck to marry you off at your age.

(LEONIDA *is about to retort when* POCHE *appears.*)

POCHE: Good evening, good evening. I'm so glad to see you.
BOURSEY: Oh. (*He lifts his handkerchief from* LEONIDA'S *shoes and pretends to be blowing his nose. Large smudges appear on his face.*) I am Theodore Boursey.
POCHE: Delighted to meet you. And where is the lovely Leonida?
LEONIDA (*lowering her eyes*): Here I am.
POCHE: Good heavens!
LEONIDA: What did you say?
POCHE: I am surprised, mademoiselle. When you filled out the prospectus, you did not do yourself justice.
BOURSEY: Be honest. There isn't a dog's chance, is there?
LEONIDA: Theodore, how dare you!
POCHE: I think there is every chance. The young lady would make a handsome wife. I think she is capable of inspiring a great passion. . . .
BOURSEY: You can say that, after seeing her?
LEONIDA: Theodore, you're a beast.

BOURSEY (*to* POCHE): Have you really got somebody who might be interested in her?

POCHE: Certainly, if all goes well.

BOURSEY: But will it? Look at her again.

LEONIDA (*to* POCHE): This is the man on whom I have thrown away my young years.

BOURSEY: I'll be only too happy if he can fix you up. But you'll have a hard time. She's a sour old bird.

POCHE: Please. Not at all.

LEONIDA: He's a wicked, spiteful man, Monsieur Poche.

BOURSEY: And a terrible problem to feed. She won't eat beef or mutton. We have all that beef and mutton left over. We have to throw it out.

POCHE: Not so loudly, please. Someone may hear you. A suitor.

BOURSEY: You've actually got a suitor out there? The poor fool.

POCHE: I have two of them.

LEONIDA (*overjoyed*): Shall I go out and see them or will they come in and see me?

POCHE: Don't be in too much of a hurry, mademoiselle. You're not exactly dressed for the part.

LEONIDA: Why not?

POCHE: You should have an evening dress, something alluring, something low-cut.

LEONIDA: I haven't got one.

BOURSEY: If we have to go out looking for an evening dress at this hour. . . .

POCHE: That won't be necessary. We have everything you need here. I'll take you to my costume mistress. By the time she's finished with you, no man will be able to resist you.

BOURSEY: Look here, if you can really take her off my hands, I'll add twenty thousand to the dowry.

LEONIDA: Theodore, darling, that makes up for all your insults. (*Kisses him.*)

BOURSEY: But only if you get married.

POCHE: With one hundred and twenty thousand francs? Inevitable. Last week I married off an eighty-year-old lady for half that amount. Everything will be fine. Now, you hurry along, mademoiselle, and get dressed.

BOURSEY: I could use a wash myself.

(*He goes out with* LEONIDA.)

POCHE: Five feet eight inches, and solid up and down. But still, 120,000 francs . . . (*Noticing the plaster on the floor.*) A lump of plaster. (*Picks it up and puts it in his pocket.*) I hope the building is safe. (*Looks worriedly at the ceiling.*) It must have broken off the cornice.

(SYLVAIN *comes in, dragging* DANNE *by the arm.*)

SYLVAIN: He's in here, Dad, and he wants to talk to you.

POCHE: Another prospect for Leonida.

SYLVAIN: This is my dad.

POCHE: Good evening, monsieur. Allow me to thank you for the confidence you have shown in me by visiting my establishment.

DANNE: They told me I could just walk in.

POCHE: Indeed you may. Some of the finest families in France are among my clientele. I spoke to your son earlier this evening. A fine, upstanding young gentleman. I can see that he takes after you.

DANNE: Yes, he's a good boy.

POCHE: Don't worry about him any more. I am going to find him a lovely wife.

DANNE: Very kind of you to put yourself out.

POCHE: Not at all. It is my work and my pleasure.

DANNE (*to* SYLVAIN):   Say thank you to the man.

SYLVAIN: Thank you. Talking about wives, there's a plump little girl in the other room. If you could dig up something along those lines . . .

POCHE: We will try. Please have a seat.

DANNE: Don't mind if I do. (DANNE *and* SYLVAIN *sit down.*)

POCHE: You've come at the right time. My register is full of bargains, some new, some not so new, some—shall we say?—used. (*Opens the creaking book.*)

DANNE (*to* SYLVAIN):   What's he opening that thing for?

SYLVAIN: To take out a few of the finest names in France.

DANNE: Have a cake. (*He takes two out of his pocket, gives one to* SYLVAIN *and eats the other himself.*) I've got cream all over my pockets.

POCHE: Now, what have we here? I never divulge names, you understand. Discretion is my hallmark. Number 2403, that's a possible match. She brings a dowry of fifty thousand francs.

DANNE: I want something better than that.

SYLVAIN: So do I.

POCHE: I'll look farther. (*He turns the pages.*)

(DANNE *reaches into his pocket for a pastry, pulls out a lump of brick, and bites into it.*)

DANNE: Ow, a brick! I've broken my jaw. (*Drops the brick.*)

POCHE: Here's number 9827. Dowry: eighty thousand francs.

DANNE: That's better.

POCHE: "Perfect health. Blameless character. Will play the piano, if desired. . . ."

DANNE: We don't go in for that kind of thing.

POCHE: There is only one drawback. She has one eye. . . .

SYLVAIN: A squint?

POCHE: No, it's a perfectly good eye. But she hasn't got another to go with it. I might as well tell you now; you'd be sure to notice it.

DANNE: We've got nothing against one eye, have we, Son?

SYLVAIN: But Dad—one eye . . .

DANNE: You see the same things with one eye as you see with two. She's not blind.

POCHE: No, wait. I've just thought of something even better to offer you. A superb woman . . .

SYLVAIN: Anything like the plump little girl in the other room?

POCHE: Very similar. And this, let me tell you, is a woman with a heart. She has given some of her early years to caring for a crotchety, arthritic old man.

DANNE: We don't mind that, do we, Son?

SYLVAIN: I haven't got arthritis.

POCHE: Dowry: 120,000 francs.

DANNE: That's for us!

SYLVAIN: Bring her in!

DANNE: Listen, what about this? My boy can have the eighty thousand francs. . . .

SYLVAIN: The one-eye?

DANNE: Yes, the one-eye. And I'll take the 120,000.

POCHE: You? By all means.

SYLVAIN: That's no good. I want a wife, not a stepmother. Besides, you're senile.

DANNE: I don't know. Sometimes, on a Sunday evening, after a day's rest, there's a lot of life in me. (*He pirouettes clumsily.*)

POCHE (*lathering his hands in air*):   So now we have two young men to marry. First, I will register you, one at a time.

DANNE: That's right, register us.

POCHE: Two hundred francs please.

DANNE: What for?

POCHE: One hundred for you and one hundred for your
son. For security.
DANNE: Let me see the girls first.
POCHE: I'm sorry. Money first.
DANNE: Girls first.
POCHE: It isn't our practice.
DANNE: Then I won't get married. Nor will my boy.
POCHE: As you wish. (*Closes his register.*)
SYLVAIN: Dad, don't stop now. Offer him half.
DANNE: Can't. Haven't got a single franc on me. It was
the police. They even took away our kitty.
SYLVAIN: But I was depending on you for my allowance.
(*He stamps out.*)
POCHE: One hundred and twenty thousand francs. Isn't it
worth two hundred?
DANNE: Not till I see the girls. Which way did my boy
go? (*Exit.*)
POCHE: A pity. Well, there are two of them left. (*Goes to
the door and beckons* CORDEN *in.*) This way, please.
CORDEN: Is she here yet?
POCHE: Yes.
CORDEN: Have you seen her? Is she a blonde? I'm par-
tial to blondes.
POCHE: No, she's a brunette. And the dowry has changed.
It has gone up from one hundred to one hundred and twenty
thousand francs. But, as I say, she's a brunette.
CORDEN: That's good. I'm partial to brunettes.
POCHE: What's this? (*He picks up the piece of brick
dropped by* DANNE.) The place is falling apart. (*He looks up
fearfully.*)
CORDEN: Anything wrong?
POCHE: That's the second one. (*Puts the brick in his
pocket.*)
CORDEN: I'm getting anxious. Present me.
POCHE: Wait here. I'll send her in.
CORDEN: How soon?
POCHE: Now. I'll see that you are not interrupted. Re-
member . . . That's strange. This whole place smells of co-
logne.
CORDEN: Don't worry about that. You were saying: "Re-
member . . ."
POCHE: Yes. Remember not to throw your chest out so
far. You're bulging again. In a different place. (*Exit.*)
CORDEN: My belt is slipping. I ought to take it off. But
someone might see. She might see. I hope she likes me. (*He
goes to the mirror.*) I wish I had time to comb my hair again.

No, it's too late. (*Enter* LEONIDA *in evening dress.*) What does she want? Hello.

LEONIDA: Hello. (*She looks about the room.*)

CORDEN: I am—expecting someone in here.

LEONIDA: So am I.

CORDEN: Your brother was looking for you before, in another room.

LEONIDA: I'll speak to him later. I haven't had a dance yet. Would you escort me into the ballroom? I don't want to go in alone.

CORDEN: With pleasure. You don't mind if I leave you afterwards? I'm going outside.

LEONIDA: Not at all.

(*They go out, arm-in-arm, just as* POCHE *comes in.*)

POCHE: Where did they get to? They couldn't have run away. They hardly met. Unless they're trying to get out of paying my commission . . .

(LEONIDA *and* CORDEN *reappear at opposite ends of the room.*)

LEONIDA: I thought you were going outside. . . .

CORDEN: I thought you wanted to dance. . . .

POCHE (*coming between them*):   Well, what have you two lovebirds been saying to each other? Is everything all right? (*They gape at him.*) Well, is it a match? (*To* CORDEN.) She's the one. (*To* LEONIDA.) He's the one.

CORDEN: What? Old Leonida?

LEONIDA: What? Fatty Corden! I don't want him.

CORDEN: I don't want her.

LEONIDA: We know each other.

CORDEN: We've been playing cards together for twenty years.

LEONIDA: Is this why you brought me all the way to Paris?

CORDEN: Is this why I hired an expensive evening jacket and outfit? I want my security back.

POCHE: Now, keep calm. This is only your first encounter. I have many others. Some of the finest names in France.

CORDEN: I'm going for my coat. I'll be back in five minutes for my money. (*Exit.*)

LEONIDA: I'm heartbroken. Let me have my dress back.

POCHE: Now wait, Mademoiselle Leonida. He doesn't

count. I have another man waiting to see you, the one I wrote to you about. A man in a very high position. Wait there.

(*He goes out.* LEONIDA *walks to the mirror, pats her hair, powders her nose, adjusts the shoulders on her dress.* POCHE *comes in with* CHUTE. LEONIDA *has her back to them.*)

POCHE: There she is, by the mirror. Good luck.

CHUTE: Good evening, mademoiselle.

LEONIDA: Good evening. (*She turns and recognizes him.*)

CHUTE: I have heard so much about you. . . . (*She turns away hastily.*) Is anything wrong?

LEONIDA: No, it's the excitement.

CHUTE: I understand. (*Aside.*) She's a big girl, but attractive. And shy. I'm sure I know her face. (*Aloud.*) Didn't I see you at the theater last Tuesday?

LEONIDA: I don't think so. I don't go to the theater. (*Aside.*) He doesn't remember me.

CHUTE: Or at the Museum of Oriental Art, perhaps?

LEONIDA: No, I don't like museums.

CHUTE: I may be wrong, but I have a good memory for faces. Especially such a pretty face as yours. I know that you have given some of your early years to caring for an old man, but I am sure that you could never have been more desirable than you are now.

LEONIDA: Thank you.

CHUTE: Were you in the Mardi Gras procession today?

LEONIDA: The Mardi Gras? What is that?

CHUTE: I've seen you very recently. I should remember where.

LEONIDA (*still turned away*):   Does it matter?

CHUTE: No, I suppose not. Would you like to dance?

LEONIDA: I don't care for dancing. Couldn't we stay here, like this, and talk?

(BOURSEY *bursts in.*)

BOURSEY: Well, how's it going? What do you think of her?

CHUTE (*recognizing him*):   Now I know you, both of you.

BOURSEY: It's the commissioner. (*He goes out again at high speed, followed by* LEONIDA.)

CHUTE: Stop! Stop those people!

(DANNE *wanders in, from the other end of the room.*)

DANNE: I'm dying of thirst. It's those pastries.
CHUTE: The other one!
DANNE: His worship! (*He rushes out again.*)
CHUTE: They're all here. The whole gang. After them!
Police, police! (*He pulls a whistle out of his pocket and blows it while he is running after* DANNE.)

ACT V

(A street in Paris. At the rear, a building under construction, with planking in front. On the left a grocery store with a sign in front: "Laiterie," and in smaller letters: "Lait—Beurre—Fromage—Oeufs Frais." To one side of the store is a fruit shop, with a sign: "Aux Halles de Paris, Fruits et Légumes." As the curtain goes up, TRICOT, the owner of the fruit store, is just opening up.)

TRICOT: What with the trumpets and fireworks and the shouting, I didn't close my eyes all night. Thank the Lord that's over for another year.

(MADAME CARAMEL comes out of the grocery store and arranges some eggs on the stand in front.)

MME. CARAMEL: Lovely morning, Monsieur Tricot.

TRICOT: Yes, but what a night it was! Bedlam, Babylon, Jericho. I see you're getting the fresh eggs out for the beginning of Lent.

MME. CARAMEL: Same as always. I picked out the biggest and freshest ones and put them aside, two weeks ago.

TRICOT: There's nothing like a fresh egg for Lent. Personally, I stick to fish.

MME. CARAMEL: You don't know what's good for you.

(Sound of a trumpet.)

TRICOT: Don't tell me they're starting up again. I'm going in. *Salut,* Madame Caramel.

MME. CARAMEL: *Salut,* Monsieur Tricot.

(She puts out a few more eggs, leaves the basket with the remaining eggs in front, and goes into her shop. One of the planks at the back is pushed aside and BOURSEY's head appears cautiously and looks to either side.)

BOURSEY: Nobody about. I'll risk it. (*Pushes his way out, past the plank.*) We spent the night in there. We had just rushed out of Poche's place when we ran into Chute, the assistant commissioner, and four of his men. Leonida almost fainted. We couldn't run carrying her, so we took shelter in this building, which is still under construction. It was my idea. All the best ideas come from me. The others are helpless. I'm the only man of action. Corden keeps groaning, and Danne keeps losing his temper. Anyway, Blanche and Leonida bedded down on some sawdust and workmen's overalls, and the rest of us slept in wheelbarrows. I'm so stiff from lying in one position all night that you could put wheels under me and trundle me away.

(CORDEN *pokes his head through the planks.*)

CORDEN: Psst, psst!
BOURSEY: What's that? Oh, it's you. You scared the wits out of me.
CORDEN: Is it clear?
BOURSEY: Yes.

(CORDEN *comes out laboriously, still wearing his evening clothes.*)

CORDEN: What a trip! My God, what a trip!
BOURSEY: You haven't stopped saying that all night. I could hear you from my wheelbarrow.
DANNE: Hisst!

(CORDEN *and* BOURSEY *spin in fright.*)

BOURSEY: Now *he's* starting.
DANNE: Is it all right to come out?
BOURSEY: Yes.

(DANNE *squeezes out. Like the other two, he is covered with plaster and dust.*)

DANNE: I've had enough of this. It can't go on any longer.
BOURSEY: What do you want to do about it?
DANNE: I protest, that's what. Sleeping in wheelbarrows, nothing to eat for dinner but pastries, cream all over my pockets, and no breakfast.
CORDEN: What a trip! My God, what a trip!

BOURSEY: Stop complaining. As soon as my sister wakes up we'll catch the first train home.

DANNE: How? They took everything away from us except our handkerchiefs, and we can't buy tickets with them. I've had enough of this. It can't go on any longer. I protest.

BOURSEY: *We* have no money, that's true, but Corden has.

CORDEN: Who says so?

BOURSEY: You weren't with us at the police station, were you?

DANNE: Of course he wasn't.

CORDEN: Excuse me, I had only 114 francs in my pocket, for personal expenses, when we left.

BOURSEY: That's enough to get us home.

DANNE: Stop arguing and hand it over.

CORDEN: It's all gone.

DANNE } Where?
BOURSEY

CORDEN: That rogue Poche took a hundred francs from me so that I could see your sister. And I'd been seeing her at the card table for nothing for the last twenty years.

BOURSEY: But you should have fourteen francs left.

CORDEN: I spent them on the belt.

BOURSEY: At least you still have your watch.

CORDEN: No, I had to leave it with the tailor who lent me this outfit. I was counting on the kitty for the money to pay him. He still has my clothes and my watch.

BOURSEY: Let's go and return the suit.

CORDEN: In this condition? And without any money to pay for the hiring?

BOURSEY: Then we're stuck.

CORDEN: What a trip! My God, what a trip!

DANNE: I've had enough of this. It can't go on any longer. I protest.

BOURSEY: We'll never get anywhere if you two keep on like that. Let's put our trust in Providence and think hard.

(They think. CORDEN *suddenly lets out a cry that makes the other two start.)*

CORDEN: Ah, look what I've found in my vest pocket: fifty centimes.

BOURSEY: What did I tell you? It's Providence.

DANNE: Some Providence. What can you do with fifty centimes for the five of us? Let me take care of them.

BOURSEY: No, they belong to the community. We'll take a vote on what to do. Who's going to speak first?

CORDEN } I am.
DANNE }

BOURSEY: Don't let's start that again. Corden, you're the oldest. Let's have your contribution.

CORDEN: Gentlemen . . . what a trip, my God, what a trip!

BOURSEY: Yes. Go on.

CORDEN: That's all I have to say.

BOURSEY: That's all I expected from you. Danne?

DANNE: I suggest we buy as much bread and sausage as we can afford with the fifty centimes.

BOURSEY: And after you've eaten—what then?

DANNE: I don't know. We'll think about it later.

BOURSEY: Neither of those suggestions gets us very far.

CORDEN: What do you expect? I'm overwhelmed by our bad luck.

BOURSEY: With me, it's the opposite. I find my true stature under conditions of adversity. I grow. I thrive on danger and difficulties. I was born for great achievements.

CORDEN: What are you going to do?

BOURSEY: First, I am going to buy a stamp for twenty centimes.

DANNE: You can't eat a stamp.

BOURSEY: That leaves thirty centimes. Then I shall write to our friend Penuri, the tax collector, and ask him to send us five hundred francs.

CORDEN: Five hundred francs!

DANNE: We're saved!

BOURSEY: Put it down to my unfailing ingenuity.

CORDEN: But wait a minute. How can he send us the money? We have no return address.

DANNE: And how can we live till the money arrives?

BOURSEY: Fellow citizens of Endives-Under-Glass, believe in me, trust me. In the old days, when I used to stay in Paris, I always put up at the Hotel Driftwood. I used to tip the people there heavily. They're sure to remember me.

CORDEN: Well?

DANNE: What about it?

BOURSEY: I'll tell Penuri to send the money to us, care of the Hotel Driftwood. In the meantime, we'll take rooms there and live comfortably until the money reaches us.

CORDEN: I'll be able to get my clothes back.

BOURSEY: What do you say to that?

CORDEN: You're a genius.

DANNE: A superman.

BOURSEY: No, I am not a superman. I merely happen to be gifted. Now I am going to buy a stamp, then I shall borrow a pen and ink, and the letter will go out by the next post. In the meantime, you two can try to wake Leonida. (*He goes out.*)

CORDEN: Yes, wake Leonida. But how? She's snoring like a trumpet.

DANNE: Wish I had a jug of cold water to tip down her back.

(BLANCHE *pushes aside the plank, and helps* LEONIDA *through.*)

BLANCHE: Careful with your dress, Aunt Leonida.

CORDEN ⎱ Here she is.
DANNE ⎰

LEONIDA (*yawning, and still in her evening gown*): Where are we? Why am I wearing this dress?

DANNE: Give her another ten minutes to come alive.

TRICOT (*coming out in front of his shop and looking at them*): What, more processions? (*He goes in again.*)

BLANCHE: I think it's raining.

CORDEN: I'm frozen. While we're waiting, why don't we find a warm store and go inside? We can look at the merchandise. It's better than standing here.

BLANCHE: Good idea. Let's find a dress shop or a china store.

DANNE: Don't buy anything.

BLANCHE: Aren't you coming with us?

DANNE: No, somebody has to wait here for your father.

CHORUS: Let us fly
Before the storm
To a store where it's dry
And clean and warm.

(CORDEN, BLANCHE, *and* LEONIDA *go off, leaving* DANNE *alone.*)

DANNE: I didn't tell the others. I have one pastry left. A bit squashed, but it's food.

(*Takes it out and eats it.* BOURSEY *appears, pursued by a waiter.*)

BOURSEY: It's only twenty-five centimes in Endives-Under-Glass.

WAITER: It's forty centimes in Paris.

DANNE: What's wrong?

BOURSEY: The post office wasn't open, so I went into a cafe to borrow a pen and ink. They said I had to buy something; I ordered a glass of sugared water, which is only twenty-five centimes . . .

WAITER: Forty centimes . . .

DANNE: Did you drink it?

BOURSEY: Yes.

DANNE: You'll have to pay him.

BOURSEY: I can't. I spent twenty of our fifty centimes on a stamp from the machine. (*To* WAITER.) Take thirty. That's all I have left.

WAITER: If you haven't got the money you shouldn't order.

BOURSEY: I'll have a little more respect from you, please. You don't even know who I am. (*To* DANNE.) Call me Commandant.

WAITER: You can call yourself major-general if you like, but you'll still pay up.

BOURSEY: Very well. You'll have to come back with me to my hotel.

DANNE (*admiringly*): He never runs out of ideas.

WAITER: Is it far away?

BOURSEY: No, it's the Hotel Driftwood.

WAITER: So you're staying at the Hotel Driftwood?

BOURSEY: I am indeed.

WAITER: That's interesting. It was pulled down twelve years ago.

BOURSEY: Oh. (*To* DANNE.) I've sent the letter off.

DANNE: Five hundred francs gone.

WAITER: You're nothing but a couple of cheap crooks.

BOURSEY: Why, you insolent young . . .

DANNE: Don't fight, don't fight!

(*He grabs* BOURSEY, *who is about to throw himself at the* WAITER, *and swings him back by the arm. Caught off balance,* BOURSEY *staggers into the front window of the fruit store. There is a tinkle of glass.*)

TRICOT (*coming outside and standing with his hands on his hips*): One broken shop window. That will be three hundred francs.

BOURSEY (*sitting on the ground*): Now we have two creditors.

(SYLVAIN *comes on the scene. His clothes are awry, his jacket is back to front. He is very drunk.*)

SYLVAIN (*singing*):
> Here is my heart, take it.
> Here is my heart, break it.
> Here is my heart, make it
> Yours . . .

DANNE: My boy. We're saved!

BOURSEY (*to* TRICOT *and the* WAITER): Now you will be paid.

SYLVAIN: Hello, Dad.

DANNE: Where's your wallet? (*Reaches into* SYLVAIN'*s pocket.*) What's this? A false nose.

BOURSEY (*reaching into the other pocket*): Here's his wallet. (*Opening it.*) Ten centimes.

DANNE: Is that all?

BOURSEY: Ten and thirty makes forty. (*To the* WAITER.) Here are your miserable forty centimes. (*The* WAITER *takes the money and goes.*) That's one debt out of the way.

TRICOT: What about my three hundred francs?

BOURSEY (*fumbling in his own pockets*): Just a moment. Let me have another look through my clothes.

DANNE: How is it you're not at the school?

SYLVAIN: I said good-by to the school. Good-by, school, I said. And now I'm going to be a waiter. I have a job at The Smiling Bull.

DANNE: You're drunk, you good-for-nothing. I'll give you Smiling Bull.

SYLVAIN: I'm still thirsty. Waiter, another glass of Beaujolais. (DANNE *gives him a furious push.* SYLVAIN *crashes into the basket of eggs.*)

EVERYBODY: Ah!

MME. CARAMEL (*coming out swiftly*): All my eggs broken, my fresh-laid eggs.

DANNE: I'll send you some more.

MME. CARAMEL: You will not. You'll pay me twenty-five francs.

BOURSEY: Now we have two creditors again, and it's worse than before.

SYLVAIN: Don't cry, old girl. You can come to my place. I haven't got any eggs, but I will give you a chair.

DANNE: His place!

BOURSEY: He has a house.

DANNE: We're saved. We'll sell his furniture. (*To* SYLVAIN.) Where do you live?

SYLVAIN: In a tall building. Ah, um, wait a minute. You go past this bridge—

BOURSEY: Which bridge?

SYLVAIN: I don't remember. Yes, I do remember. I live at number 118.

DANNE: What street?

SYLVAIN: That's hard. I don't know that.

DANNE: Idiot!

BOURSEY: Animal!

SYLVAIN: I'm not comfortable here. (*He staggers over to a bench, sits down, and falls asleep. Some cries are heard from nearby.* CORDEN, LEONIDA, *and* BLANCHE *pant in.*)

DANNE: What's happening?

CORDEN: A crowd of children were chasing me and shouting: "Scarecrow, scarecrow, feed him to the birds."

LEONIDA: And when we went into a dress shop, the woman thought I was a tourist and said: "Madame, you're a day late for the carnival."

CORDEN: What a trip, my God, what a trip!

TRICOT: How much longer are we supposed to wait?

BLANCHE: What do these people want?

TRICOT: My window.

MME. CARAMEL: My eggs.

BOURSEY: I'd forgotten about them. (*He starts to fumble in his pockets again.* DANNE *does the same.*) How are we ever going to get out of this? (*Suddenly, looking at* LEONIDA.) I know a way.

DANNE: We're saved.

CORDEN: What is it?

BOURSEY: Leonida . . . her diamond pendant . . . they forgot to take it.

DANNE: Of course. We can sell it.

CORDEN: No.

LEONIDA: No.

BOURSEY: I know how you feel. It was a present from Corden when you were a godmother and he was a godfather. But we can't think about that now. Give it to me. I'll run to the nearest jeweler and get what I can for it.

CORDEN: Stop! It's useless.

EVERYBODY: Why?

CORDEN: I don't know how to tell you. It's not a diamond. It's an imitation. . . .

EVERYBODY: Paste! False! A hoax, etc.

CORDEN: It's not my fault. I was in a hurry. I didn't have time to look for a diamond.

LEONIDA: You cad!

DANNE: You rat!

BOURSEY: You blackguard! No man of honor would give a lady an imitation diamond.

CORDEN: Anyway, I couldn't afford a real one.

TRICOT: I'm not going to waste all day waiting for you.

MME. CARAMEL: Pay us now or . . .

BOURSEY: Give us another minute. (*He and* DANNE *make a pretense of going through their pockets again.*)

TRICOT: Not another second. I'm going to call my friend, the assistant police commissioner.

EVERYBODY: The commissioner!

DANNE: His worship!

BOURSEY: No, please, I beg of you—

(FELIX *enters.*)

FELIX: At last! Here you are.

EVERYBODY: Felix!

DANNE: *We're saved!*

BOURSEY (*to* FELIX): My boy, we're delighted to see you. My daughter is yours. Now.

BLANCHE: Thank you, Father.

FELIX: Thank you, Father.

BOURSEY: And now—have you any money?

FELIX: Why, yes.

EVERYBODY: He has money!

BOURSEY: Pay these people for me. Twenty-five francs to this woman; three hundred francs to this man.

FELIX: Blanche . . .

BOURSEY: Pay them now.

FELIX: Certainly. I don't know what this is all about, but still . . . (*He gives* TRICOT *and* MME. CARAMEL *the money, and they go back into their shops.*)

CORDEN: It's lucky that you turned up.

FELIX: I've been looking for you since yesterday morning. I've been to every monument and park in Paris. Last night I was watching the procession, hoping to see you when I spotted the thief.

EVERYBODY: What thief?

FELIX: The thief who took my watch on the boulevard yesterday. I recognized him immediately, and grabbed him just as he was putting his hand into somebody else's pocket.

BOURSEY: Did you get your watch back?

FELIX: No. He said he'd thrown it into somebody's umbrella.

BOURSEY: Mine. My umbrella.

DANNE: So that's how it got there. This time we really are saved.

BOURSEY: They'll have to admit we were innocent.

CORDEN: They'll have to give us back the kitty.

BOURSEY: Felix, my daughter is yours.

FELIX: Thank you, thank you. (*He goes to take* BLANCHE'*s hand.*)

BOURSEY (*pulling* BLANCHE *away*): But first, have you any money?

FELIX: More money?

BOURSEY: To pay for lunch. We haven't eaten yet.

SYLVAIN (*waking up*): Lunch? Very good, monsieur. I'm going to be a waiter.

DANNE: You'll wait in the cowshed. I'm taking you back to Endives-Under-Glass. I'll make a farmer of you yet.

BOURSEY: After lunch we'll pay a visit to our friend the commissioner.

DANNE: I'll ask him for my pickax.

BOURSEY: He will give us our kitty back and this time we'll celebrate at home.

CORDEN: Yes, with a bouncing great turkey buried under truffles.

FELIX
BLANCHE } No, a ball. . . .

DANNE: No, the fair at Cressy. . . .

BOURSEY: Order, order! We'll put it to the vote. Who wants to speak first?

EVERYBODY: I do!

BOURSEY: We'll decide when we get back. Now, gentlemen, give your arms to the ladies and we will all go to lunch.

EVERYBODY: To lunch!

CHORUS (*they sing*):
> So it's good-by to Paris,
> The big, bad city,
> Which tried to embarrass
> Us out of our kitty.
> Before another day can pass
> We'll be back in
> > back in
> > back in
> Dear old Endives-Under-Glass.

GEORGES COURTELINE
(1858–1929)

Georges Courteline was as dedicated a fighter as his younger contemporary, that master of ringcraft, Georges Carpentier. "What a pleasure it would be," he once wrote, "to use physical force in a good cause. To stop a taxi and give the driver your address. To let him tell you, 'It's twenty francs,' and reply: 'That's all right.' To get into the cab. To arrive. To tell the driver as you're paying him: 'Here are the three francs, fifteen centimes registered on your meter, plus thirty-five centimes for your tip.' To wait for the result. To watch him scramble out of his seat, with his eyes shining like a wild animal's, then to break his arm with one clean blow, and go indoors to join the family for dinner."

As it happened, Courteline was a physically small man, and there is no record of his ever having broken a taxi driver's or anybody else's arm with one blow, clean or otherwise. Nevertheless, he was a fighter. Almost all his plays—he wrote twenty-eight, most of them one-acts—are attacks: on bureaucrats, on pompous and pretentious people, on hypocrites, and other villains who make comedy worth writing.

Courteline is the nearest modern equivalent to Molière, who was his idol. Like Molière, he let out his anger and frustration by means of satirical comedy. Like Molière, he preferred to write realistically, with only occasional touches of extravagance—there is hardly a reader or spectator who will not recognize every one of Courteline's situations, and who will not have clashed with at least one of his characters. Like Molière, he wrote "tight" plays, wasting hardly a word. But if Courteline was neither as prolific nor as penetrating a writer as Molière, he is nearer to our time, and his plays are funnier for us to watch than the comedies of many recent French dramatists, simply because Courteline kept sentimentality in the wings. He wanted to make his audiences laugh, not gulp.

If he had tried to convert his stage to a pulpit, he might not be worth our attention today. As it is, Courteline, who died in

1929, reads and plays like a contemporary. His "Complete Works" have been published and republished in France, and new productions of his plays appear every year. There were three of them showing in Paris when I spent a season there some years ago, including the one in this collection, *The Commissioner Has a Big Heart*, which provided a relaxing romp for the Comédie-Française company, after five rigorous and almost motionless acts of Corneille's *Cinna*.

The Commissioner is a good introduction to Courteline. One of his favorite themes was the conflict between abstract or ideal justice on the one hand and, on the other hand, manmade law, as manipulated by lawyers and functionaries. In this play, the law, personified by the Commissioner, is trodden down and humiliated by a madman. This is, of course, a wishful, wistful idea: something Courteline would have *liked* to see, just as he would have liked to snap the taxi driver's arm. It is a situation that never happened; yet reading or watching the play, we are convinced that it *could* have happened. In spite of the farcical elements in the play, there is no point at which we can say: "This is impossible."

The character of the Commissioner may well be filtered down from the first tyrant Courteline ever met, a schoolmaster under whom he suffered for several years at Meaux:

"I had a teacher in the fourth grade whose name was Grangé. This man took pleasure in martyring me. I may have been a cancer to him—and I don't deny that I was—but a poor, defenseless cancer. He took advantage of my defenselessness by torturing me.

"One day, when I was talking in class, he gave me one thousand lines to copy out, as a punishment. Do you realize what that means—one thousand lines? A day's work, an entire Sunday. But there it was. The following Monday I handed in my thousand lines.

" 'I told you to do a thousand lines of *Latin*,' my executioner remarked. 'You'll have to do them over, my lad.'

"A thousand lines of Latin! That meant another entire Sunday copying out of the first hundred lines of the *Aeneid* ten times.

"But that wasn't the end. The next day, I gave my forced homework to Monsieur Grangé. Can you imagine what that miserable man said? 'I ordered you to copy out one thousand *different* Latin lines, sir, and not the same one hundred lines ten times over. Do it again.'

"Grangé, that was his name. Grangé. The monster."

The bulk of Courteline's drama was written between 1890 (when he was thirty-two) and 1910, and later revised, word for word. Almost all his plays are based directly on his own experiences: his knocks at the civil service come from his thirteen years as an official in the Ministry of Culture; his army plays from his two years in Hussars; his leg-pulling of the law courts from some personal, drawn-out tangles with the French legal system and also from his father's work as a recorder at the tribunal in Tours; and his plays about the inscrutability of women were provoked by a couple of "let-downs" during his bachelor days in Montmartre.

The realism—which is the essence of the humor—in Courteline's writing, attracted the great naturalistic director, André Antoine, who first encouraged Courteline to write for the stage, and who produced most of Courteline's famous plays, notably *Boubouroche, Article 330, Afraid to Fight, Hold On, Hortense, The Commissioner Has a Big Heart,* and a dozen or so others. From what we know of Antoine's pro-ductions, they did not try to stretch the farce. Courteline is a lot more entertaining when his characters look and talk like real people. A director who plants phony mustaches on his actors' upper lips and makes them behave grotesquely will rob both his audiences and casts of laughs.

As a realist, Courteline had anything but an indulgent view of his fellow men. But he was not a pessimist. He was aware of their weaknesses, and bore down on them—hard. "Man is not wicked," he wrote in his last book, *The Philosophy of Georges Courteline.* "He is foolish, spiteful, boastful, unkind, stupidly skeptical and at the same time credulous . . . as insolent as a pageboy or as cowardly as a flea, depending on whether he is up against somebody weaker or stronger than himself; he is as helpless at managing his own affairs as he is ready to butt into other people's . . . he will play the piano with one finger, so that he knowingly prevents writers from writing, invalids from resting and dying people from passing on in peace . . . But he is not, I repeat, wicked, in the exact sense of the term. . . ."

Out of this indignation came pure comedy. The writer Maurice Barrès told him: "When I read your writings I laugh like a monkey. . . ."

A LIST OF COURTELINE'S PRINCIPAL PLAYS:

Lidoire* (1891); *Boubouroche* (1893); *Afraid to Fight** (1894); *A Serious Client** (1896); *Hold on, Hortense!** (1897); *Badin the Bold** (1897); *The Hidden Correspondence** (1897); *A Registered Letter** (1897); *Theodore Can't Find His Matches** (1897); *Problems, Problems** (1897); *The Overturned Coach** (1897); *These Cornfields** (1898); *The Pitiless Policeman** (1899); *The Commissioner Has a Big Heart** (1899); *Article 330** (1900); *The Balances** (1901); *Victories and Conquests** (1902); *Peace at Home** (1903); *The Conversion of Alceste** (1905); *The Blockhead* (1909).
* Plays in one act or one scene.

SUGGESTIONS FOR FURTHER READING
ON COURTELINE:

See the introduction by the present translator to *The Plays of Courteline* (New York: Theatre Arts Books, 1960), and the entry on Courteline in *The Reader's Encyclopedia of World Drama* (New York: Thomas Y. Crowell, 1969). Three *saynètes*, one-scene plays, translated by Jacques Barzun, are in *Tulane Drama Review*, October 1958; Eric Bentley's translation of *These Cornfields* appears in *Let's Get a Divorce and Other Plays* (New York: Hill & Wang, 1958); and five other plays, one translated by Jacques Barzun, four by Albert Bermel, are included in *The Plays of Courteline*.

IN FRENCH ONLY:

La Curieuse Vie de Georges Courteline by Albert Dubeux (Paris: Pierre Horay, 1958). Courteline's collected works in French are now available in several editions.

THE COMMISSIONER HAS A BIG HEART

A Comedy in One Act

by Georges Courteline
(in collaboration with Jules Lévy)

FIRST PERFORMED IN PARIS IN 1899

CHARACTERS
(in order of appearance)

POLICE COMMISSIONER
A GENTLEMAN
A POLICEMAN
M. PUNEZ (*Puny*)
A LADY
BRELOC
FLOCHE
TWO POLICEMEN (*Lagrenaille and Garrigou*)

*Note: the first Policeman can be
played by Lagrenaille or Garrigou.*

The office of a local police commissioner in Paris. On the right is a window which can be opened, on the left a small door leading into a coal closet. At the back of the stage is a double door—the entrance to the office—and to the left of this door a fireplace with a fire burning.

COMMISSIONER (*at his desk*): Now don't keep pestering me. I have other people waiting.

GENTLEMAN: Please, all I want is a license to carry a gun.

COMMISSIONER: No.

GENTLEMAN: What difference does it make to you?

COMMISSIONER: The answer is still no.

GENTLEMAN: It's dangerous in my neighborhood. We're swarming with crooks who fight all night and pounce on anybody passing by. People are being robbed. And because of my job I don't get home until late each night.

COMMISSIONER: Find another job.

GENTLEMAN: You find it for me.

COMMISSIONER: What do you think this is—a placement bureau?

GENTLEMAN: Look, Commissioner, suppose someone attacks me tonight?

COMMISSIONER: Come and report it to me tomorrow.

GENTLEMAN: And then what?

COMMISSIONER: Then I'll give you a license to carry a gun.

GENTLEMAN: I see. I don't have the right to protect my skin until somebody's already blown holes in it.

COMMISSIONER: That's right.

GENTLEMAN: Some police force! Some protection!

COMMISSIONER: That's enough. Keep that kind of talk to yourself. I do what I'm told. I'm here to explain the law, not to defend it. If you're not satisfied with our institutions, change them.

GENTLEMAN: If it was up to me . . .

COMMISSIONER: What's that? One more word and I'll have you inside. Who do you think you are, stirring up discontent and revolution right in the commissioner's office. You're lucky I have a big heart. (*The man starts to speak.*) That's enough,
155

I said. Get out of here and make it quick before I change my mind. (*The man disappears swiftly.*) Another anarchist! Have to watch out for him. (*Comes back to his desk, pulls a pile of folders toward him—the morning's mail, sorted out by a clerk —and skims each one in turn. He frowns and rings his bell. A policeman appears.*) Ask Puny to come in here. (*Policeman goes out and almost immediately Punez appears, a man of fifty or so, timid, withdrawn, unable to disguise his fear of the world. He takes off the cloth cap that hides his skull and comes hesitantly forward, making small deferential gestures all the way.*) Good morning Monsieur Puny. Once again I must inform you that you do your work with the cleanliness and efficiency of a pig. If this goes on, I shall be compelled to ask the prefect to dismiss or demote you. Hundreds of times, Monsieur Puny, I've told you to go through my mail ruthlessly, so that I can get my desk, my work and my thinking clear. And what happens? I might as well whistle through my ears for all the good it's done. Look at this. (*He picks out a sheet of paper at random.*) "Complaint by a chambermaid about her employer, who tried to take advantage of her." What's this got to do with me? Get rid of it. (*He takes another sheet.*) "Complaint by a certain party against a cabdriver who used foul language." Amazing. Is this supposed to be for *my* attention? Get rid of it. (*Takes another sheet.*) Here's another one. A janitor with lazy ears and a tenant who had to wait for two hours in the rain. Let him talk to the landlord. I'm not a porter. Get rid of it. And here's a cook who's owed a week's wages. That's for the magistrate to settle, not me. And so is that. And that. And that. Get rid of them all. It looks to me, Monsieur Puny, as if you're wrapped up in dreams of love, or else I've over-estimated your intelligence. This is the last straw. (*Punez starts to speak.*) Silence! I may have a big heart, but I won't have you taking advantage of me. Let this be a lesson to you. It's your last chance, for sure. Good morning, Monsieur Puny.

PUNEZ (*humble and smiling*):   I am of Spanish origin. My name is pronounced Poon-yez. (*He bows to the ground and goes out.*)

The Commissioner goes back to work, importantly stamping his papers. Re-enter the policeman.

COMMISSIONER: Next one. (*Policeman goes out.*) Fire's almost out. (*Gets up.*) It's like Siberia. (*Goes to the coal closet, gets a coal brick and feeds it to the fire. At that moment a lady comes in.*)

LADY: Are you the commissioner?

COMMISSIONER: I am.

LADY: I've come to complain . . .

COMMISSIONER: About your husband.

LADY: Why, yes.

COMMISSIONER: A good guess, wasn't it? Well, I can't do anything for you, Madame. Sorry, but I have too much to do.

LADY: Sir . . . (*She goes to sit down.*)

COMMISSIONER: Please, don't sit down, Madame. It's useless. You'll only be wasting your time and mine. It's strange how seventy-five percent of you women expect the police commissioner to be able to mend your broken marriages. Don't you realize that family squabbles are not within my jurisdiction? I cannot, I *must* not intervene, except in flagrant cases of adultery, when a third party—a mistress, for example—has wrecked a household. Is that what your husband has been up to?

LADY: Sir . . .

COMMISSIONER: No more useless talk, Madame. Let me have a straight yes or no.

LADY: But . . .

COMMISSIONER: If it's yes, submit a regulation complaint to the public prosecutor, who will pass on instructions to me. If it's no, you have no valid plea, and you may as well go home.

LADY: My husband is not deceiving me.

COMMISSIONER: What *is* he doing, beating you? If so, you'll need witnesses, then you can institute divorce proceedings, and the judges will decide in your favor. I have no idea why you women insist on coming to me with your bickering. You don't think about me, do you? If I had to carry an olive branch into the middle of every scrap between a husband and wife, I'd need forty hours a day and sixty days a month.

LADY: But Commissioner, that's not the trouble. My husband doesn't beat me, and he isn't playing around with other women.

COMMISSIONER: What's wrong then? Perhaps he's out of his mind?

LADY: That's it, exactly.

COMMISSIONER: Madame, I have better things to do than sit here and make jokes with you.

LADY: But it's true. How did you guess?

COMMISSIONER: I'm used to this kind of thing. Believe me, I know your story by heart, from A to Z. I hear it ten times a day. Would you like a piece of advice, good advice? (*She nods.*) Go home quietly and start making dinner. Your husband is no more out of his mind than I am.

LADY: Oh, yes he is. He's a raving lunatic.

COMMISSIONER: He isn't.

LADY: He is. He ought to be locked up.

COMMISSIONER: Does he drink?

LADY: Never.

COMMISSIONER: Has he ever had typhoid fever or sunstroke?

LADY: Not to my knowledge.

COMMISSIONER: Does he come from a family of alcoholics, epileptics or mentally defectives?

LADY: I don't think so.

COMMISSIONER: Well, there you are.

LADY: Where? Just because there's no lunacy in his family, what does that prove?

COMMISSIONER: Listen to me . . .

LADY: He doesn't drink—so what? That doesn't stop him acting like a madman, saying things I can't make head nor tail of, doing things he doesn't even understand himself.

COMMISSIONER: What kind of things?

LADY: Every night I hear him brooding, making plans and threats, muttering to himself—to say nothing of his leaping out of bed in his nightshirt, with a revolver in his hand and shouting: "I'll blow out the brains of any man who touches my wife." Is that a natural way to behave, I ask you?

COMMISSIONER: He's jealous.

LADY: Jealous!

COMMISSIONER: Of course.

LADY: Tell me, then, is he jealous when he locks himself up in a cupboard for two or three hours at a time, and rants at the top of his voice, attacking society, screaming that the universe has a spider on its ceiling, a bug in its bedstead and a rat in its bass violin?

COMMISSIONER (*amused*):   He really says that? A rat in its bass violin?

LADY: His very words. And that's not all. He calls everybody else crazy. He marches up and down, shouting: "One, two; one, two!" He says it's good for the lungs. He's become the laughing-stock of the neighborhood. The children march along behind him, shouting "Here comes the village idiot."

COMMISSIONER: You're exaggerating.

LADY (*anxiously*):   I'm not.

COMMISSIONER: Come now. If that were true, one of my patrolmen would have pulled him in long ago for disturbing the peace.

LADY (*bitterly*): All the patrolmen seem to worry about is telling the street-vendors to move on.

COMMISSIONER: My patrolmen are hard-working fellows; they know what they have to do and they do it. If you're trying to take it out on them, you've come to the wrong place. I may have a big heart, but don't think I'm going to put up with any of your impudence. Let's settle this business about your husband once and for all. You still insist that he's crazy. All right, he's crazy.

LADY: Well, then . . .

COMMISSIONER: Well, then, what do you want me to do about it?

LADY: I thought . . .

COMMISSIONER: You were wrong. I'm not a psychiatrist. I can't cure him. You'll have to take your husband's case— if there is a case—to the Welfare Commission, not to me. And short of a miracle, they won't do anything for you either.

LADY: Why not?

COMMISSIONER: Women—they always want to know the answers. Because, Madame, the Welfare Commission is a lot poorer than people think. It simply can't cope with all the requests that come in to it.

LADY (*standing up*): In that case, Commissioner, I must warn you: up to now my husband has only been a danger to me; but before long he'll be a danger to everybody.

COMMISSIONER: When that times comes, Madame, you can be assured that we shall think about it. In the meantime, first, the asylums are overflowing with patients and swamped with new requests for admission. Second, I can't lock up a man whose hallucinations exist only in the mind of his wife. And finally, I can't afford to spend a whole afternoon in a pointless discussion. Your best plan is to let things remain exactly as they stand. (*He gets up.*)

LADY: One more thing, Commissioner . . .

COMMISSIONER: You're a charming conversationalist, Madame, with all sorts of interesting ideas, but unfortunately, duty calls, as they say in the operas, and I must bid you good afternoon. Tell your husband to try bromides, long walks and hydrotherapy. (*Calling out*) Show this lady out.

The Lady goes out. The Commissioner gets back to his papers, but is again interrupted . . .

OFFSTAGE VOICE: Commissioner!
COMMISSIONER: What is it?
VOICE: Can you spare me one minute?

COMMISSIONER: You're sure that's all?

VOICE: One minute, no more.

COMMISSIONER: One single minute?

VOICE: I promise.

COMMISSIONER: All right . . . (*He gives in. Enter Breloc, who takes off his hat.*) What can I do for you?

BRELOC: Nothing complicated, I just wanted to hand in this watch which I found last night on the corner of boulevard Saint-Michel and rue Monsieur-le-Prince.

COMMISSIONER: A watch?

BRELOC: A watch.

COMMISSIONER: Let me see it.

BRELOC: Here. (*He takes it from his pocket and hands it to the Commissioner, who examines it closely.*)

COMMISSIONER: It certainly is a watch.

BRELOC: No mistake about it.

COMMISSIONER: Thank you. (*He goes to his table and puts the watch in a drawer.*)

BRELOC: Well, I'll be going.

COMMISSIONER: Not yet.

BRELOC: I'm in a bit of a hurry.

COMMISSIONER: I'm sorry about that.

BRELOC: I have somebody waiting outside.

COMMISSIONER: They'll wait.

BRELOC: But . . .

COMMISSIONER: You don't think I'm going to take this watch off your hands before you tell me how it got there in the first place?

BRELOC: I've already told you, sir. I found it last night on the street corner.

COMMISSIONER: Yes, but where?

BRELOC: On the ground, of course.

COMMISSIONER: On the sidewalk?

BRELOC: On the sidewalk.

COMMISSIONER: That's ridiculous. The sidewalk is no place to put a watch.

BRELOC: May I say that . . . ?

COMMISSIONER: You may not. I think I know my business best. I'd better take down your particulars.

BRELOC (*becoming impatient*): My name is Breloc, Jean Eustache. I was born at Pontoise on the 29th of December, 39 years ago. I am the son of Pierre Timoléon Alphonse Jean Jacques Alfred Oscar Breloc and Céleste Breloc, née Moucherol, his wife.

COMMISSIONER: Your address?

BRELOC: 47 rue Pétrelle, rue Pétrelle second floor—directly above the mezzanine.

COMMISSIONER (*writing it down*): Your income and property?

BRELOC (*angrily*): I have 25,000 livres annually, a farm in Touraine, an estate in Beauce, six dogs, three cats, a donkey, eleven rabbits, a wild boar from India . . .

COMMISSIONER: That'll do. What time exactly did you discover this watch?

BRELOC: Three o'clock in the morning.

COMMISSIONER: It that all?

BRELOC: Yes.

COMMISSIONER: It seems to me that you lead a peculiar life.

BRELOC: It's my life and I'm very satisfied with it.

COMMISSIONER: Maybe, but there's one thing you haven't explained. What were you doing at three o'clock in the morning on the corner of Le-Prince when you *say* you live at 47 rue Pétrelle?

BRELOC: I say it because it's true.

COMMISSIONER: We'll see about that. I have some more questions to ask you, and from now on I expect civil answers. What were you doing so late at night in a strange neighborhood?

BRELOC: I'd been to see a—a lady friend.

COMMISSIONER: What does she do, this lady friend?

BRELOC: She's married.

COMMISSIONER: To whom?

BRELOC: A pharmacist.

COMMISSIONER: His name?

BRELOC: That's my business.

COMMISSIONER: Are you talking to me?

BRELOC: I think so.

COMMISSIONER: Now look here, mister, you'd better change your tone. I don't like it one bit, and I don't like your face any better, is that clear?

BRELOC: Too bad.

COMMISSIONER: I expect cooperation around here. Now have you ever been charged with a criminal offense?

BRELOC: Have you?

COMMISSIONER (*jumping up*): I won't have this insolence.

BRELOC: You're a goddam fool.

COMMISSIONER: Take that back.

BRELOC: You make me sick. What do you take me for, a crook?

The next two speeches are spoken simultaneously, with Breloc's sentences running into those of the Commissioner, and vice-versa.

BRELOC: I've just about had my fill of you, with your damn-fool questionnaire. I never heard of such a thing. I find a watch in the street. I put myself out to bring it to you and this is the thanks I get. This has been a lesson to me. In future when I find something it goes in my pocket and stays. No more messing around with the goddam police force.
COMMISSIONER: Don't start with me, my lad. You'd better look out. I'll soon teach you how to talk to me properly. Who the hell are you? You tell me you live on rue Pétrelle. Prove it. You say your name is Breloc. How do I know if you're telling the truth? There's only one way to settle this . . .

He runs across and opens the door.

COMMISSIONER: Take this man away and throw him in the cooler. (*Policeman enters.*)
BRELOC: For God's sake. This is about the limit.
POLICEMAN: Come on, come on. No backchat.
BRELOC (*as he is being dragged out*): You wait! Just let me find one more watch, that's all. Just one more . . . (*He disappears.*)
COMMISSIONER: He calls himself Breloc—who knows what his real name is? If I wanted to, I could be a Breloc myself. If you listened to them, they'd *all* call themselves Breloc. (*Going to the window.*) It's freezing in here. There's a draught coming in this window.

There are shouts outside. The doors open violently and Floche stands there, between two policemen.

FLOCHE: The Commissioner. Where's the Commissioner? I want to have a word with the Commissioner.
COMMISSIONER (*to policemen*): What's wrong with him?
FLOCHE: Are you the Commissioner?
COMMISSIONER: Cut out that noise. Speak when I tell you to. Lagrenaille, what's it all about?
LAGRENAILLE: This man was creating a disturbance, sir, at a crowded intersection. Abusing the Republic and so forth. People were running over to listen and holding up traffic, so Patrolman Garrigou here and I stopped and asked him politely to move on. He refused, so we took him into custody, without violence.

COMMISSIONER: Was he preaching revolution?

LAGRENAILLE: No, sir.

COMMISSIONER: Did he injure you?

LAGRENAILLE: No, sir.

FLOCHE: I had no reason to be unpleasant with the patrolmen. As for revolution, I want to say here and now that I have too much respect for authority to dream of such a thing.

COMMISSIONER: Then why didn't you do what you were told?

FLOCHE: When?

COMMISSIONER: When the policemen asked you to move on.

FLOCHE: Oh that.

COMMISSIONER: What do you mean, "oh that?"

FLOCHE: "Oh that" means "oh that." What else could it mean? Everybody has a right to say "oh that" if he wants to.

COMMISSIONER: Yes, but you don't have the right to start public demonstrations of a seditious character at the top of your voice.

FLOCHE: I'm disgusted with the Republic.

COMMISSIONER: That's no reason to make others disgusted.

FLOCHE: How about that! (*He laughs.*)

COMMISSIONER: How about what?

FLOCHE: Have I said something wrong?

COMMISSIONER: Yes, you have. Go on talking to me like this and you'll soon see a change of scenery. (*To the policemen.*) You can go. (*They leave.*) "How about that!" What an expression. (*He takes a fresh sheet of paper, dips his pen in the ink.*) Your name?

FLOCHE: Floche.

COMMISSIONER: With or without an S?

FLOCHE: Without.

COMMISSIONER: Given names?

FLOCHE: Jean Édouard. Address: 129 rue des Vieilles Haudriettes.

COMMISSIONER: Work?

FLOCHE: Don't have any. I have a little capital which works for me.

COMMISSIONER: Any decorations?

FLOCHE: Who, me? No.

COMMISSIONER: What about that? (*He points to a wide red ribbon, resembling the ribbon of the Legion of Honor, in Floche's lapel.*)

FLOCHE: Oh, that? Just a reminder. (*Laughs.*) I have a terrible memory. It goes out on me. I keep it under control with this ribbon. It reminds me of what I have to do . . . where I'm going . . . you know. It's my own idea and it works very well, much better than a knot in a handkerchief, which you forget about until you catch cold. And it's better than a pin in your sleeve, which makes you look a fool because people laugh at it.

COMMISSIONER: It won't make the judges laugh, I'll tell you that. More likely to get you six months in jail. Take it off. (*Floche puts the ribbon away.*) Your age?

FLOCHE (*sitting down*): Do you realize what it's like for a poet who's trying to write a tragedy in the same room as a piano teacher who practices scales from morning to night? (*The Commissioner's mouth opens.*) No? Well, my memory is like that poet. It works in the same brain as a genius that is making too much music.

COMMISSIONER: You're making a nuisance of yourself. No more of this fancy language; just answer my questions. How old are you?

FLOCHE: Twenty-five.

COMMISSIONER: What was that?

FLOCHE: Twenty-five.

COMMISSIONER: Twenty-five? You're only twenty-five?

FLOCHE: Yes.

COMMISSIONER: You mean you *were* twenty-five.

FLOCHE: I was and I am.

COMMISSIONER: Doesn't make sense.

FLOCHE: Yes, it does. It's as logical as algebra, as clear as moonlight, as simple as the soul of a child. I *was* twenty-five, of course I was, and on that very day I said to myself: "This is a fine age. I'm never going to change it." And I didn't. I was twenty-five, I am twenty-five and I shall *be* twenty-five until the day I die—if it's all right with you. (*Pause.*)

COMMISSIONER: Are you trying to fool me?

FLOCHE: Do I look, do I sound, do I act, as if I would do such a thing?

COMMISSIONER: Well, it's more that . . .

FLOCHE: I expected you to query that. It's only natural at a time like this, when reason staggers through the streets with its head to the ground and its legs in the air. Gradually we've got into a state when it's no longer possible to tell the true from the false, the dark from the light, the sun from the moon. And so common sense is taken for madness. That's why my wife, who lives and breathes in this insane atmosphere, has gone insane and wants to have *me* put away in an institution. (*He chuckles over that.*)

COMMISSIONER: Could it be the same . . . ? Does she have a bug in the bedstead?

FLOCHE: Right! And a rat in the bass violin.

COMMISSIONER (*aside*): I should have known. (*Aloud.*) Monsieur . . .

FLOCHE: Poor woman. She's the same as all the others. You can imagine how they all try the patience of a man of logic—dare I say a moralist?—like myself. I have decided to make a full study of the effects and causes of this decay in moral values, in a work entitled: "Mental Daltonism . . ."

COMMISSIONER: Sir . . .

FLOCHE: A work, I may say, of a high philosophical character . . .

COMMISSIONER: Of course, but . . .

FLOCHE: The fruit of my reflections, which in turn are the offspring of my long studies . . .

COMMISSIONER: Now, listen . . .

FLOCHE: And which I will now take the liberty of developing for your benefit at full length. . . . (*Interrupts himself.*) Excuse me . . . (*Gets up and goes to the door at the rear.*)

COMMISSIONER (*aside*): He's getting me worried. Why is he closing the door? (*Hurries across to the door, but Floche is now coming back, smiling to himself.*)

FLOCHE: You see? I like to make myself at home.

COMMISSIONER: Not for long, you don't. Give me the key.

FLOCHE: Which key?

COMMISSIONER: My key.

FLOCHE: You have a key?

COMMISSIONER: The key to that door.

FLOCHE: What about it?

COMMISSIONER: Give it to me.

FLOCHE (*gently*): No.

COMMISSIONER: You will.

FLOCHE: I will not.

COMMISSIONER: Why not?

FLOCHE: Because I like it better in my pocket. There's no reason why you should want the door open, and I prefer it closed. You're a public official so I'm going to confide in you. I'm going to let you in on the secret of the gods. But I wouldn't dare reveal it with that door swinging open. It would be like throwing my secret to the first inquisitive ear that happened to float by. Monsieur, the winds of madness that blow everywhere are set in motion by that kind of an indiscretion, by the misunderstanding between Nature, which commands, and Man, who does not obey; between the good intentions of the former and the misguided responses of the latter.

COMMISSIONER (*with the desperate bravery of a coward jumping into a river*): If you don't give me back that key this instant, I'll call for help and have the door broken down. Then I'll see you're tied up like a sausage and taken away to the asylum. Do you understand that?

FLOCHE: Perfectly. (*He pulls a revolver out of his pocket and levels it at the Commissioner.*) If you say one word, if you make one movement, if you take your eyes off me for one second, I shall shoot you through the nose six times and turn your face into a broken tomato. I'm dangerous when I have to deal with madmen.

COMMISSIONER: Are you calling me a . . . ?

FLOCHE: Shut up, or you'll be sorry. I may have a big heart but I don't like madmen.

COMMISSIONER (*terrified*): I appreciate that, I really do . . .

FLOCHE: The lunatic is my natural enemy . . . I hate him. I have a grudge against him. Do you follow me? The sight of a lunatic is enough to drive me out of my mind. And when I get one in my hands, I don't know what I'm doing. I'm capable of anything.

COMMISSIONER (*aside*): This is the end. It's white sheets and a slab for me. (*The two men stare at each other. Plainly, the Commissioner wouldn't give two cents for his chances. But at the moment when he has given up the ghost, Floche breaks out laughing.*)

FLOCHE: You know, for a Commissioner, you've really got the shakes.

COMMISSIONER (*who has no idea what's going on*): I have?

FLOCHE: Yes, you're terrified.

COMMISSIONER: I assure you . . .

FLOCHE: Don't make excuses. You're shivering like a plate of jelly. Couldn't you even see that I was having a game with you? Do I look like a man who would be capable of an ugly deed?

COMMISSIONER: Of course not. But . . .

FLOCHE: But what?

COMMISSIONER: That revolver. It's so easy for accidents to happen, as they say.

FLOCHE: What they say is childish nonsense. A weapon is only dangerous in the hands of a bungler, and I can control mine the way a writer controls his pen or an orator his tongue. Do you know I can shoot the spot out of an ace at 25 feet and shoot the bowl off a pipe in a man's mouth before you can count up to four?

COMMISSIONER (*feigning interest*): Really?

FLOCHE: Yes, really. I'll show you.

COMMISSIONER· What? What are you going to do?

FLOCHE: You'll see. Don't move an inch. (*He steps back a few paces, trains his revolver on the Commissioner and cocks the trigger.*)

COMMISSIONER (*who has lost his polite curiosity*): No, no!

FLOCHE: Don't keep moving, you fool! I told you there was no danger. The bullet will shave your left ear. You'll hear the whistle; it's very interesting and unusual. Ready? One, two . . .

COMMISSIONER (*jumping up and down like a goat*): No, please! I don't want to. I don't want to.

FLOCHE (*suddenly going from calmness to anger*): Blockhead, dolt, imbecile! I was ready to fire. I would have punctured you. (*Beside himself.*) When you have people like this, it's better for society to destroy them. (*He takes a long thin blade out of his walking stick.*) I don't know what stops me from pinning you to the wall like a butterfly, with twenty good inches of steel through your gut.

COMMISSIONER (*crouching behind his table*): Is it starting again? After the bullet, the blade? Well, let's get it over with. This is driving me mad.

FLOCHE: Ah! You admitted it. You're a lunatic.

COMMISSIONER: No.

FLOCHE: You're a bell with no clapper, a tree with no base, a head with no brain.

COMMISSIONER· I swear that you've misunderstood me, you misjudge me.

FLOCHE: Don't tell me what I understand. You're a typical, traditional, *classical* lunatic. You preach and tell others they're mad. You poor idiot. Every breath that comes out of your mouth is tainted with insanity. You're mad, from the clownish way you dress to the indescribable absurdity of your face.

COMMISSIONER (*timidly*): Thank you.

FLOCHE (*striding to the table*): What's all this rubbish? Is it any use?

COMMISSIONER: Yes!

FLOCHE: No. Another of your hallucinations. (*He sweeps up the pile of legal documents on the table and flings them all over the room, crumpling some, tearing up others.*)

COMMISSIONER: Oh, no, no, no!

FLOCHE (*stopping in front of the filing cabinet*): And these files. They're no good either.

COMMISSIONER: Please, please!

FLOCHE: Illusions, nightmares! (*He pulls the files out of their compartments and lets them flutter—instructions, orders, correspondence, memoranda—all over the floor. The Commissioner groans in consternation. Floche suddenly notices the fire.*) And that!

COMMISSIONER: What?

FLOCHE (*pointing to the fire*): That!

COMMISSIONER: It's a fire.

FLOCHE: A fire. (*Laughing like an epileptic.*) A fire in January!

COMMISSIONER: Why not?

FLOCHE (*to audience*): Is he a fool? No? Don't you know that, unless you're a fanatic, you only light a fire during the middle of summer?

COMMISSIONER: But why?

FLOCHE (*solemnly*): Because Nature—which is always right—decrees that man shall be hot in summer and cold during the winter. Put out that fire.

COMMISSIONER: No.

FLOCHE (*not joking*): Do you refuse?

COMMISSIONER (*persuaded*): No. (*He gets up and walks slowly toward the fire. A pause.*)

FLOCHE: Hurry! (*The Commissioner hurries. He takes a water jug off the mantel and tips it over the flames.*) Nature has also ordained that during the winter man shall be exposed to death from lung congestion, galloping tuberculosis, pleurisy, pneumonia and other related ailments. Open that window.

COMMISSIONER: No.

FLOCHE (*threateningly*): Do you refuse?

COMMISSIONER: No. (*He takes a few short steps toward the window.*)

FLOCHE: Stop slouching. Get a move on! (*The terrified Commissioner throws the window wide open.*) And finally, Nature commands that man shall have frozen feet. Take off your size thirteens.

COMMISSIONER: Oh, no, please.

FLOCHE (*leveling his revolver*): Do you refuse?

COMMISSIONER: No. (*Takes off his shoes reluctantly: speeds it up when Floche impatiently waves his revolver. He places the shoes in the corner, side by side, neatly. But Floche seizes them and tosses them out the window. He looks out with satisfaction . . . then catches sight of the coal closet.*)

FLOCHE: What's that?

COMMISSIONER: The coal closet.
FLOCHE: Good. Get in.
COMMISSIONER: Excuse me?
FLOCHE: I said: "Get in."
COMMISSIONER: But . . .
FLOCHE: Do you refuse?
COMMISSIONER: No.

Resigned and abject, the Commissioner opens the door hesitantly and looks inside. Floche grabs him by the collar and pushes him in, closes the door after him and locks it.

Then he takes his hat from the Commissioner's desk, pats the crown into position and stamps the brim with the Commissioner's stamp. He puts it on. Flicks a speck of dust off his sleeve, and marches up and down, shouting. "One, two; one, two!"

Opens the door, nods politely to the two policemen outside and leaves.

After a pause, Patrolman Garrigou comes in and looks around.

GARRIGOU: Lagrenaille, Lagrenaille!
LAGRENAILLE: What's up?
GARRIGOU: Where's the boss?
LAGRENAILLE: Don't know.
GARRIGOU: Look at this place.
LAGRENAILLE (*spotting the Commissioner's hat*): There's his lid.
GARRIGOU (*pointing to the coat*): There's his camel-hair.
LAGRENAILLE (*pointing to the umbrella*): There's his parachute.
GARRIGOU: Where's he gone? (*They rush about, bending, peering, searching right and left.*)
LAGRENAILLE: Out the window! (*They go and look.*)
GARRIGOU: Not a sign.
LAGRENAILLE: No.
GARRIGOU: It's got me beat.
COMMISSIONER'S VOICE: Lagrenaille.
LAGRENAILLE: Did you hear that?
COMMISSIONER'S VOICE: Garrigou.
GARRIGOU: Did somebody call?
COMMISSIONER'S VOICE: I'm in here.
LAGRENAILLE: The boss.
GARRIGOU: So help me, I think he's in with the coal. (*He runs across to the closet and opens it. The Commissioner bobs*

out, like a jack-in-the-box, his face covered with coal dust.)

COMMISSIONER: The maniac, the maniac! Get ropes. Get straitjackets. Get chains. Get the paddy wagon. Get the fire brigade. Get the army. The city's in danger. There's a maniac at large!

Curtain